LIBRARY CONSORTIA

ALA Editions purchases fund advocacy, awareness,
and accreditation programs for library professionals worldwide.

LIBRARY CONSORTIA

Models for Collaboration and Sustainability

Valerie Horton and Greg Pronevitz

An imprint of the American Library Association

Chicago   2015

CARLSBAD
CITY LIBRARY
Carlsbad, CA
92011

021.64
LIB

© 2015 by Valerie Horton and the Massachusetts Library System.

Printed in the United States of America

19 18 17 16 15   5 4 3 2 1

Extensive effort has gone into ensuring the reliability of the information in this book; however, the publisher makes no warranty, express or implied, with respect to the material contained herein.

ISBNs
978-0-8389-1218-8 (paper)
978-0-8389-1248-5 (PDF)
978-0-8389-1249-2 (ePub)
978-0-8389-1250-8 (Kindle)

Library of Congress Cataloging-in-Publication Data
Library consortia : models for collaboration and sustainability / [edited by] Valerie Horton and
   Greg Pronevitz.
     pages cm
 Includes bibliographical references and index.
   ISBN 978-0-8389-1218-8 (softcover : alk. paper)—ISBN 978-0-8389-1249-2 (epub)—
ISBN 978-0-8389-1248-5 (pdf)—ISBN 978-0-8389-1250-8 (kindle)
1. Library cooperation—United States 2. Library cooperation—United States—Case studies.
I. Horton, Valerie.
II. Pronevitz, Greg.
   Z672.13.U6L53 2015
   021.6'4—dc23   2014016667

Cover design by Kimberly Thornton. Image © Tomislav Forgo / Shutterstock, Inc.
Text design and composition in the Quadraat OT and Lato typefaces by Ryan Scheife / Mayfly Design.

⊗ This paper meets the requirements of ANSI/NISO Z39.48-1992 (Permanence of Paper).

NOVEMBER 2014

Contents

_____

Case Studies

Acknowledgments

We owe much gratitude to the colleagues who assisted us and contributed to this work, and acknowledge them here in the order in which their contributions appear in this book. A brief biographical sketch for each author is found after the conclusion.

We began research for this book by surveying our consortial colleagues. We thank the 77 who did respond. We focused on the 66 US respondents. We also had 11 international consortial responses. Jeanette Smithee, Southeast Florida Information Network (SEFLIN), was kind enough to work with us to expand on her responses to create a case study of SEFLIN's experiences after the 2008 recession, which can be found in chapter 2.

Discovery to delivery is such an integral part of consortial services in most organizations that we included chapters devoted to both discovery and delivery. Tracey Leger-Hornby, formerly of Worcester Polytechnic Institute, and Lori Ayre, of the Galecia Group, brought the experience and talent to make chapters 5 and 6 possible.

As we examined the consortial landscape and found sustainability to be a key issue, we felt that those directly involved in this important issue would be best equipped to write about the service projects that contributed to sustainability and member library success. We called on colleagues to prepare case studies of innovative projects to share with our readers and we are grateful for their efforts. These contributions are outlined in the overview of the case studies.

—Greg Pronevitz and Valerie Horton

CHAPTER 1

Library Consortia Overview

Valerie Horton

"The idea that libraries should, in some way, find means of work cooperatively . . . is a deeply rooted concept in librarianship."

J.W. KRAUS

No library stands alone. Library cooperation goes back to the 1880s and is a long-standing tenet of the profession. Collaboration is strongly rooted in most of our current activities. Even Harvard University has stated that no library is big enough or rich enough to go it alone anymore. In these days of scarce public resources, there is a strong belief that libraries need to justify every tax dollar received and that collaboration helps libraries extend the value of every dollar spent.

The Council on Library and Information Resources has detailed many recent collaborative efforts in its report *Higher Ground: Building a Strategic Digital Environment for Higher Education*. The report states that "the next two decades could witness an extraordinary fluorescence of activity among universities and colleges focused on repositioning, consolidation, and convergence." Collaboration is not just flourishing in academia, but also in public libraries as demonstrated by the number of libraries joining cooperatively managed e-book systems. Further, a new journal, *Collaborative Librarianship*, had over 250,000 articles downloaded in its first five years. The tool that libraries most often use to launch and manage collaborative projects is the library consortium.

This book covers the history, current landscape, management, critical trends, and key services that define today's library consortium. The book was written to help new library staff understand the full range of activities that take place in a modern consortia and to help consortia managers, participants in consortial governance, and participating libraries look for ways to revise current practices, expand services, or adopt new project ideas.

Chapter 2 highlights the current trends impacting consortia and the fiscal difficulties many have experienced since the 2007–2009 Great Recession. Chapters 3 and 4 look into current management trends and give an overview of wide-ranging consortia activities. Chapters 5 and 6 look at a key trend, the discovery-to-delivery continuum that allows us to maximize our patron services. Consortia's vital role in discovery to delivery is highlighted in these chapters. Finally, the 16 case studies selected for this book explore both the core services of consortia, such as support for integrated library systems and training, and new services, such as e-book technology and delivery methods.

In the spirit of library cooperation, we seek to share our 70 years of experience in libraries, including over 35 years managing five different library consortia in four states. We believe our experiences together with these important case studies will help the reader understand the dynamic and even revolutionary activities of today's library consortium.

What Is a Library Consortium?

"The word "consortium" is a good word for libraries. . . as it combines the past with the present and the future."

JAMES KOPP

Groups of collaborating libraries are called cooperatives, networks, collectives, alliances, and partnerships as well as consortia. The term *consortium* has been common in library literature for about 50 years. Clearly defining a library consortium can be a challenge given the diverse missions, roles, and memberships of these organizations. According to the U.S. *Code of Federal Regulations*, Sect. 54.500, a library consortium "is any local, regional, or national cooperative association of libraries that provides for the systematic and effective coordination of the resources of school, public, academic, and special libraries and information centers, for improving services to the clientele of such libraries." Dictionary definitions tend to focus on the "association" aspect of consortium, and on the goal of achieving some result beyond the resources of any single member.

Library consortia are as varied as the libraries they serve. Some consortia are international (OCLC), national (LYRASIS), regional (AMIGOS Library Services), or statewide (OhioLINK, Ohio's academic network). Others serve smaller geographic regions or a single metropolitan area, such as Metropolitan Library Service Agency (MELSA). Library consortia range in size from huge—in 2012 OCLC had 22,599 members—to the very small, such as the Flatirons Library Consortia, which has three members. Consortia can be geared towards one type of library or serve multiple types of libraries. Consortia also vary from informal groups to government-sponsored organizations to nonprofit incorporated entities. Library consortia taxonomies can be based on governance structure, geographic service area, or the type of libraries served. This book looks at all types of library consortia and gives examples from many different types and sizes of organizations.

The activities of consortia are as varied as their types and sizes. These activities tend to focus around the following clusters of activities:

Components of Discovery to Delivery

- resource sharing, interlibrary loan, online and physical delivery
- shared offsite storage, cooperative collection development, serials exchange coordination, shared e-book collections
- shared integrated library systems, technology and networking support and service, Internet service provider
- digitization programs and hosting digital assets, institutional repositories

Group Purchasing Activities

- shared database purchases, cooperative purchasing of supplies, materials, and equipment

Library Empowerment Activities

- training, continuing education, professional development, consulting

Other consortia services include virtual reference, library marketing and graphic materials creation, advocacy, human resources management, fiscal support, publications or e-mail group support, videoconferencing, meeting-room facilities, and summer reading programs. The next chapters and the case studies will go into more detail about consortia activities.

Consortia History

"The history of library cooperation is as long as the history of professional librarianship in America."

ADRIAN ALEXANDER

The American Library Association (ALA) was an early pioneer of collaborative library work. In 1876, ALA formed the Committee on Cooperation in Indexing and Cataloguing College Libraries. ALA also supported shared collections acquisition by 1913. The first interlibrary loan code was adopted in 1917. By World War II, librarians had shifted their focus to creating national and regional union catalogs. These union holding lists were important projects for library cooperation over the next thirty years.

In 1972, the U.S. Department of Education commissioned the first study to try to understand how the new cooperative models were developing. The *Directory of Academic Library Consortia* listed 125 academic consortia that had been formed since 1931; 90 percent of them were created after 1960. The study found that the need to streamline cataloging and to introduce rudimentary automation systems were the driving forces in early library consortia development. In 1996, James Kopp argued that many of the activities of the early consortia, such as reciprocal borrowing, interlibrary loan, union catalogs creation, and delivery services, were still taking place.[1]

The Triangle Research Libraries Network (TRLN) was an early and illustrative consortium. TRLN was founded in 1933 to share cataloging and collections between Duke University, North Carolina State University, and University of North Carolina. Later North Carolina Central University joined. Given their close proximity, the libraries have coordinated their materials acquisitions over many decades, enabling them to build collections that were up to 70 percent unique. TRLN was also at the forefront of many pioneering efforts in resource sharing and licensing of online resources. TRLN's Principles of Cooperation state the organization's focus is to develop a comprehensive shared collection as well as integrated discovery and delivery. TRLN is deepening its commitment to collaboration by working on shared digital initiatives, joint staffing models, and cooperatively held remote collections.

During the heyday of consortia development in the 1960s and 1970s, three large-scale bibliographic utilities were created: OCLC, the Western Library Network (WLN), and the Research Libraries Information Network (RLIN). All three organizations provided online access to bibliographic databases, which libraries used for cataloging, acquisitions, reference, and interlibrary loan. By 2006, RLIN and WLN had merged with OCLC. Multistate networks were also formed in this era, many in support of OCLC activities. These networks included Amigos Library Services, NELINET, PALINET, and Minitex. Many of these networks started as academic-only consortia but later expanded membership to serve all types of libraries.

The 1970s were also when regional library systems were developed, with about half the states creating these systems. Some regional systems were defined by the types of library they served. For instance, New York created separate systems for school, public, and academic libraries. Other regional systems had a mission to serve all types of libraries within a specific geographic area. In many states, the regional systems were charged with expansion of public library service into underserved rural areas. Most regional systems focused on library development and projects that were bigger than any one library could handle alone, such as a regional cataloging center or a shared resource-sharing system. Regional systems activities included consulting, technology assistance, joint online catalogs, and continuing education.

From the 1990s through the first decade of the twenty-first century, a second wave of consortia growth took place, driven by Internet access to online resources and databases. Along with this second wave of new consortia creation, many established consortia became larger both in budgets and in the number of participating libraries. By negotiating for group purchasing with database vendors, many of the existing multistate consortia and networks grew into mega-consortia, managing database access for hundreds, if not thousands, of libraries. One example is the Big Deal packages that focused on acquiring vast numbers of costly scholarly journals for hundreds of libraries at the same time. In contrast, niche consortia were also being created at this time to meet the needs of small, more unique groups of libraries. Niche consortia are typically small and serve a specific function, such as delivery, or have a limited geographic setting, such as metro-area libraries only, or they provide specialized online resources such as medical resources.

In 2007, a large ALA study of 240 consortia found a strong and growing library consortia landscape. The *Library Networks, Cooperatives, and Consortia Survey* (LNCC) found that consortia were defined as regional (61%), local (26%), or statewide (12%) boundaries.[2] Most consortia in the survey were multitype and were within clearly defined geographic limits. The five chief services found in that 2007 survey were:

1. Resource sharing/interlibrary loan
2. Communication
3. Professional development/continuing education
4. Consulting and technical assistance
5. Cooperative purchases (primarily databases)

Other less frequently mentioned services included automation (networking, technical support, and online catalogs), advocacy, information and referral services, courier and online document delivery services, support for standards, support for special populations, professional collections, rotating or shared collections, and digitization.

The Great Recession hit in late 2007, and library consortia headed for a period of retrenchment. Research for this book found that 21 percent of consortia surveyed in the LNCC have closed or merged. Among the big news stories during this time was the collapse and merger of several former OCLC service networks into LYRASIS and the closure of others.

Less well known was the devastating loss of regional library systems across the county. Details of those closures can be found in chapter 2. After the recession government funding was scaled back, causing many consortia to lose some or all federal or state funding. As libraries lost their funding base, they found it increasingly difficult to continue participating in cooperative ventures. By 2009, librarians were warned that "consortia cannot survive if 'business as usual' is the mandate during this economic downturn."[3] Conversely, a number of new international consortia had formed during this period. It is a paradox that library consortia are needed most in hard economic times to leverage library spending, but they are also most vulnerable at those times.

The authors of this book conducted a study of consortia, which is detailed in the next chapter. They found some good news. As the American economy improved over the past few years, fewer consortia closed. Some of the merged consortia are doing well, sometimes picking up new work from the closure of nearby organizations. Also, new consortia continue to be formed as economic pressures drive more libraries to collaborate. However, this is still a difficult time for library consortia, as public funding options remain limited and grants will only take an organization so far. It is likely that the next decade will continue to be a time of struggle for library consortia, and further consolidation is possible.

Why Do Libraries Join Consortia?

"I firmly believe that collaboration . . . is crucial to the continued success of libraries."

THOMAS A. PETERS

Libraries have myriad reasons for joining consortia. In 2012, OCLC surveyed over 100 consortia managers for its report *U.S. Library Consortia: A Snapshot of Priorities & Perspectives.* Professional networking was considered the most valuable aspect of joining a consortium by 30 percent of managers who responded, while 23 percent thought cost saving was the most valuable. In a recent Minitex survey of its stakeholders, many respondents mentioned the value of networking, commenting about how the cooperative should "bring libraries together" and "facilitate conversations . . . to share ideas about what we are all doing locally," and "stay focused on bringing people together." In the press of too much to do and too little money to do it with, managers can forget how important networking time is for library staff and how well suited library consortia are to provide this function.

From a philosophical perspective, libraries join together to advance research and learning as well as to expand access to wider resource pools. Other reasons to cooperate include sharing continuing education and obtaining expertise in high-cost staff areas such as technology. Prestige can play a role as well. Academic libraries that join the Committee on Institutional Cooperation (CIC) gain both prestige and access to a wealth of resources and supported services. Many libraries are members of numerous consortia; for example, North Carolina State University is a member of nine different consortia, Atlanta University Center belongs to seven, and Claremont College Library belongs to five. This proliferation of participation in consortia is not without detractors. Paula Kaufman, a dean at the University of Illinois at Urbana-Champaign wrote, "My institution belongs to so many [consortia] that it is nearly a full-time job to sort out what products and services each offers at what price and with what conditions."[4]

There are many reasons to cooperate, but one of the most critical reasons to join a library consortium is to obtain economies of scale. The Big Deal packages that group hundreds of academic libraries into negotiations with scholarly journal vendors is one of the strongest examples of libraries gaining substantial saving through cooperation, though these deals also are not without their detractors. The digitization efforts through HathiTrust could not be accomplished without 100 institutions pooling their resources, nor would the pioneering work of the Digital Public Library of America (DPLA) be possible without the contributions of many library consortia.

In 2011, Marshall Breeding in his annual automation marketplace article predicted that we would see greater participation in ever larger integrated library systems (ILS) run by consortia. Breeding's prediction has been validated by public libraries in Colorado. Prior to 2009, 34 percent of the state's public libraries were part of a shared ILS or a union catalog system; by 2013 that number was over 60 percent. There are significant advantages to a library in joining a shared catalog, including a decreased need for in-house equipment or staff expertise, access to an integrated resource-sharing system, and learning and sharing the wisdom of the collaborative.

Any review of the literature will quickly show that joining a library consortium is not always cheaper. Collaboration is time consuming and can be a drain on staff time and resources. For instance, one library consortium may offer a top-of-the-line, vendor-based integrated library system while another consortium offers a less expensive and less developed open-source system such as Koha or Evergreen. The cost of membership in these systems is substantially different. A number of academic libraries have formed a consortium to create an academic, high-end, open-source integrated library system called Kauli Ole.

The development costs for such a system are high, but the participating organizations gain a system in which they control the design and development of the product. Cost is not the driving factor for all libraries that participate in shared activities, but it is one of the most important considerations.

As previously stated, consortia are not without their detractors. Kaufman has raged that the time and energy spent dealing with consortia issues can be a mini-nightmare. Library literature is replete with articles from the late 1990s and early 2000s on the inefficiencies of some early library consortium projects.[5] Major criticisms include the confusing number of consortia database offerings, too many meetings, too little agreement, too much time required, and too many delays in launching new technology-based systems. Additionally, many directors have expressed concern about joining a consortia effort when those efforts may not be sustainable, thereby creating a self-fulfilling prophecy.

Interestingly enough, in the past ten years a counterargument has developed. Many library leaders are now saying that the mistake made by those earlier pioneers was not putting in enough time or resources into cooperative efforts. While there is evidence that passive collaboration fails, we are seeing increasing evidence that deep collaboration succeeds. In an editorial for *Collaborative Librarianship*, this author defined deep collaboration as "two or more people or organizations contributing substantial levels of personal or organizational commitment, including shared authority, joint responsibility, and robust resources allocation, to achieve a common or mutually beneficial goal."[6]

If one looks at some of the new deep collaborative projects, such as Kauli OLE, DPLA, or HathiTrust, one can see direct evidence of success. Further, consortia such as TRLN and Orbis Cascade are gaining profound new levels of deep cooperation from their members. Library directors are now saying we need to commit more time, money, and staff resources if we wish to transform libraries to meet the demands of the new information era.

Conclusion

Library consortia have been through periods of growth and retrenchment. Remaining relevant to participating libraries is one of the most crucial considerations for library consortia. Many consortia are at the forefront of deep collaborative projects that are transforming the library landscape. It is the power of the collective that allows for projects with enough scope to change the norms under which have libraries have operated for a long, long time. Consortia allow a place for experimentation and change, and allow creativity to be unleashed and explored.

Today's consortia are far from the glorified buying clubs they were in the past. Chapter 2 highlights many services that libraries receive from consortia, proving that consortia activities have become crucial for many libraries. Library cooperatives help libraries become more productive and offer more resources to patrons. In the end, the reason so many libraries join together is to achieve more than any library can achieve on its own. The era of the library consortia is not ending; instead it is set for a transformation as technology has removed many of the physical barriers to collaboration that distance formerly created.

Notes

1. James Kopp, "Library Consortia and Information Technology: The Past, the Present, the Promise," *Information Technology & Libraries* 17, no. 1 (March 1998).
2. Denise Davis, "Library Networks, Cooperatives and Consortia: A National Survey," *ALA Report* (December 3, 2007), www.ala.org/offices/sites/ala.org.offices/files/content/ors/lncc/interim_report_1_may2006.pdf.
3. Katherine Perry, "Where Are Library Consortia Going? Results of a 2009 Survey," *Serials* 22, no. 2 (July 2009): 126.
4. Paula A. Kaufman, "Whose Good Old Days Are These? A Dozen Predictions for the Digital Age," *Journal of Library Administration* 35, no. 3 (2001): 13.
5. Thomas A. Peters, "Consortia and Their Discontents," *Journal of Academic Librarianship* 29, no. 2 (March 2003).
6. Valerie Horton, "Going 'All-in' for Deep Collaboration," *Collaborative Librarianship* 5, no. 2 (2013): 66.

CHAPTER 2

The Consortial Landscape

Greg Pronevitz

Results of 2012 Survey of US Consortia at a Glance

- More than 200 consortia operate across the country.

- At least 65 consortia closed or merged since 2007 and no longer operate.

- Minitex is the largest consortium (4,250 participating libraries).

- BC Electronic Library Network is the smallest consortium (2 libraries).

- Average membership is 236 libraries; median membership is 53 libraries.

- Aggregate membership exceeds 18,000 libraries.

- The average budget is $2.9 million; the median budget is $1.2 million.

- The aggregate budget exceeds $170 million.

- Average staffing level is 9.6 FTE; median staffing level is 6 FTE.

To understand the consortial landscape, the authors of this book conducted research in 2012 and looked at existing studies. They sent an online survey, Library Consortia in the 21st Century, to several e-mail lists used by library consortia personnel to gather data. The survey is referred to as "our 2012 survey" or "our survey" to differentiate it from a 2012 OCLC survey noted later in the chapter. The authors were particularly interested in the effect of the 2007–2009 Great Recession, the challenges presented during and after the subsequent slow recovery, and the variety of services provided by consortia. Responses from 77 library consortia were tabulated. The focus of this chapter is on the 66 responses received from consortia in the United States.

Membership in the 66 responding US consortia comprises more than 18,000 libraries. Sixty of those consortia reported budget figures; the aggregate of those exceeds $170 million per year.

In 2007, 240 library consortia were identified in the comprehensive survey Library Networks, Cooperatives and Consortia: A National Survey, by Denise M. Davis of the Office of Research and Statistics at the ALA. This study was supported with funding from the Institute for Museum and Library Services, enabling researchers to track down non-respondents and tabulate large data sets. The authors of this book found that 190 of the original 240 consortia still exist, though some as merged organizations. This analysis indicated that 50 consortia, or about 21 percent, are no longer operating.

Sixty-six US consortia responded to our 2012 survey, including 28 new consortia that were not included in the 190 mentioned above. Mergers and closings of consortia since 2008 were driven by two major factors that resulted in an overall reduction of 65 known consortia nationwide. The economic crisis brought on reductions in state funding of regional systems, leading to numerous mergers and closures in California, Illinois, Massachusetts, New Jersey, and Texas. The realignment of OCLC services and network support was the second major factor leading to seven service providers merging into others or closing.

Mergers accounted for the closings of five regional library systems in Massachusetts and the renaming of the sixth as a statewide organization, the Massachusetts Library System. Similarly, four regional library systems in New Jersey became LibraryLinkNJ. In Illinois, nine systems were merged into two, while in California fifteen consortia were merged into eight. In Texas only two of ten regional library systems are still in operation.

A number of former OCLC service provider networks are also no longer in operation. NEBASE in Nebraska merged with BCR, a mountain states service provider, BCR subsequently closed. NYLINK in New York also closed. NELINET in New England, Pennsylvania's PALINET, and SOLINET in the southeast merged to form LYRASIS. Indiana's INCOLSA and the Michigan Library Consortium merged to form the Midwest Collaborative for Library Services. MLNC in Missouri merged into Amigos Library Services in the Southwest. Amigos also took on work formally done by some of the closed Texas regional library systems. Two other OCLC-related groups that were included on the ALA list became part of OCLC itself. The new merged OCLC service networks continue to provide some OCLC services as well as other services to thousands of libraries. ILLINET (Illinois), Minitex (Minnesota and the Dakotas), OHIONET, FEDLINK (federal libraries), and WiLS (Wisconsin) also continued to provide some OCLC services.

There is variation in how members were counted. The largest consortia reporting is MINITEX with 4,250 participating libraries, and the smallest is the BC Electronic Library Network with two libraries. The average membership is 236, and the median membership is 53. The average staffing level is 9.6 full-time equivalents (FTEs) with a median staffing of about six. Staff with an MLS or equivalent average is 4.1 FTE; other professional staff averages 3.4 FTE. The average annual budget is $2.8 million with a median budget of $1.2 million. Responses were received from 31 states. The state with the highest participation rate was Massachusetts, with six consortia responding. Three states—California, New York, and Ohio—each had five consortia responding. The remaining responses included no more than three consortia per state.

To understand the effects of the economic downturn, our 2012 survey asked an open-ended question: "Has your consortium undergone any major changes since 2007 such as a merger, serious cutback, membership decline, or closure?" The most common major change reported was budget reductions. A total of 22, or 33 percent, of respondents noted budget reductions. On the other hand, two consortia noted budget increases.

Surprisingly, 16 respondents (24 percent) reported the major change was an increase in membership. Looking deeper into the explanations provided by some respondents, we found that these membership increases occurred because new libraries join consortia either to take advantage of online content discount programs or to join shared integrated library systems. Two consortia noted that they gained members when a nearby consortium closed or merged. It is also interesting to note that five consortia mentioned a membership loss, and one of those explained that the loss was made up by new members.

Consortial staff reductions, organizational restructuring, service additions, and many service eliminations were noted by multiple respondents. Three consortia also noted recent mergers. As expected, closed consortia did not respond.

Thirty-three unique consortial respondents listed funding and related issues as both a current and a long-term challenge. Our survey included two questions about significant issues faced by library consortia. The first question was: "Please describe the most significant current challenges that your consortium is facing." Twenty-five consortia listed the following issues as major challenges: funding/revenue generation, budgets, and sustainability.

The second question was: "Please describe any major long-term challenges that you believe will affect your members and/or your consortium." The survey did not include check boxes about current and future challenges. Since more than half of the respondents answered this question, the authors concluded that they were correct in their hypothesis that the economic downturn was still strongly affecting library consortia. Seven consortia reported declining funding from membership as a challenge. On the other hand, six consortia reported increased funding or activities. Additional issues raised included insufficient staffing (listed by six consortia), physical delivery (listed by three), library staffing, small libraries, and school libraries.

Services

The most widely offered services provided by US library consortia, as listed by more than 50 percent of respondents were:

- training
- shared electronic content
- group purchasing
- physical delivery

The next most common services, offered by 24 to 50 percent of respondents, were:

- consulting
- shared integrated library system (ILS)
- mediated interlibrary loan for returnable items
- cooperative collection development among members
- shared digital repository
- mediated document delivery of nonreturnable items

The chart below illustrates the range of services and the respective percentages offered by US library consortia. Many of these services play a part in the discovery-to-delivery process that is covered in depth in chapters 5 and 6.

FIGURE 2.1. Services Provided by US Consortia as Percent of Total Respondents

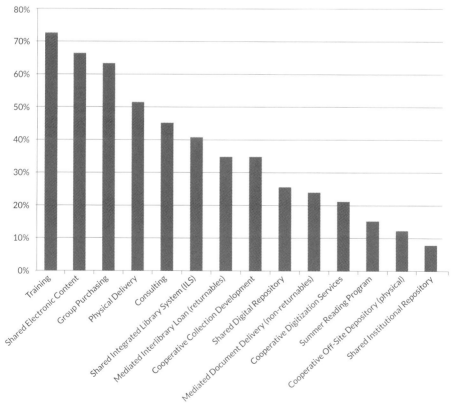

Membership

The aggregate library membership of the 66 responding US consortia is 18,142, with an average membership of 236. Median membership is 53 libraries, with 34 percent of respondents citing membership exceeding 100 libraries. Public library consortia comprised more than half, or 34, of responding consortia. Academic consortia were the second largest group of responders, with 21 returning surveys. Six of the academic consortia included either the state library or a handful of other members with academic libraries constituting the vast majority of members. Nine respondents were from multitype consortia, and two were statewide school library consortia.

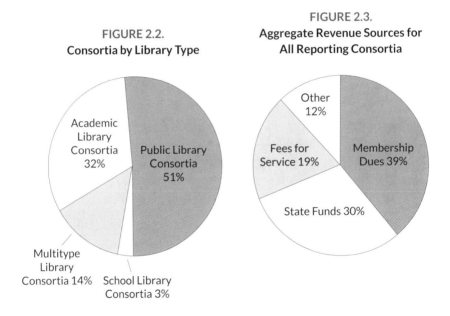

FIGURE 2.2.
Consortia by Library Type

Academic Library Consortia 32%

Public Library Consortia 51%

Multitype Library Consortia 14%

School Library Consortia 3%

FIGURE 2.3.
Aggregate Revenue Sources for All Reporting Consortia

Other 12%

Fees for Service 19%

Membership Dues 39%

State Funds 30%

Budgets and Revenues

Our 2012 survey included questions about annual budgets and sources of revenue. Of the 60 consortia that reported annual budgets, the highest was $23,700,000 and the lowest was $3,000. The average budget was $2.9 million, with the median budget about $1.2 million.

The survey asked consortia to provide information about their sources of revenue, and 54 respondents gave the following information to illustrate aggregate funding sources:

- membership dues revenue: 39 percent
- state funding: 30 percent
- fees for services: 19 percent
- other sources (often LSTA and other grants or cost sharing): 12 percent

Membership dues income is the most significant revenue source for 17, or 31 percent, of respondents. For 12 consortia, membership dues comprised more than 90 percent of their overall funding.

State funds are the most significant funding source for 11 consortia, or 20 percent, and comprise 30 percent of the aggregate funding. The economic crisis that began in 2007 led to state budget cuts, and 8 of the 11 consortia that rely heavily on state funding indicated that they had to cut staff and services because they lost some state funding.

Mergers and Consortial Collaboration

Consortia in five states merged or closed at least partially as a result of the 2008 economic crisis. As noted above, the simultaneous realignment of the relationships between OCLC and service networks, as well as the economic crisis, led to the closing or merger of nine OCLC service networks. Three OCLC networks expanded due to the mergers.

Consortia in other states are taking the following steps to work together to improve services and efficiencies.

- New York's nine 3Rs regional library systems recently published a study on the potential for statewide collaboration, including steps planned for working together, in I2NY: *Envisioning an Information Infrastructure for New York State*, which can be found at www.ny3rs.org/wp-content/uploads/2012/11/Final-report-5_20_2013.pdf.

- Wisconsin's 17 library systems completed a study of the role of library systems, how to increase their relevance through collaboration and service standards, and the impact of possible mergers, which was reported in *Creating Effective Systems*, found at www.srlaaw.org/2013Process/CreatingEffectiveSystems8-2-13.pdf.

Interstate physical delivery, which is only possible when consortia work together, has been in place for over a decade in Minnesota, Wisconsin, and the Dakotas and for five years within Colorado, Kansas, and Missouri consortia. Massachusetts also has a joint project, noted in our survey, in which three shared integrated library systems are working together on an Evergreen open-source ILS platform. In Florida multiconsortial collaboration includes a shared discovery platform and the development of webinars for statewide access.

Two collaborative projects of note that allow multiple consortia to leverage their strengths include Califa and its Enki e-book platform for hosting and delivering libraries' digital content (see Case Study 2, The Enki Experiment) and the wide deals sponsored by LYRAIS and the Center for Research Libraries (CRL). The wide deals allow multiple consortia to benefit from the negotiations for expensive scholarly journals and other electronic content by major players in consortial agreements (see Case Study 5, Embracing Wide Deals).

In Massachusetts the merger of six regional library systems into a single statewide organization was necessary following drastic state budget cuts in 2010. Some benefits of consolidation emerged. The merged organization is better suited for making statewide decisions. This has led to increased buying power for electronic content through a single bid process in collaboration with the state agency. On the other hand, some libraries lost access to local content that was very important to them because they lost local regional system support. One of Massachusetts' challenges is to develop a statewide model to assist libraries in securing licenses for local content.

An additional example of statewide collaboration in Massachusetts is a planned statewide e-book platform (see Case Study 3, Statewide E-book Project for Multitype Libraries in Massachusetts). This project grew out of a call to action following a statewide program on resource sharing hosted at the joint expense of the state library agency and the statewide consortium. Funding such an event and reacting quickly to the call for action would not have been as straightforward under a system with multiple regional systems that each had separate budgets and decision-making priorities. Massachusetts' challenge now is to ensure that all libraries are able to benefit from this statewide program and that no one loses sight of the need to support traditional resource sharing as it embarks on this new venture.

Strength in Numbers

Library consortia must focus on the needs of their own local audience. This is a financial imperative because membership dues, state funds, and fees for service sustain these organizations. There are situations, however, when working on a larger scale can benefit members and consortial organizations. Determining the right size is not always based on rational or logical bases. Geography often guides such decision-making. However, when it comes to joining forces with other consortia, logical measures are employable.

Economy of scale or coherence of scale is worthy of consideration when planning consortial services and projects. The Council on Library and Information Resources and Vanderbilt University partnered to form the Committee on Coherence of Scale in 2012. The Committee is considering correlation among several consortial projects, including the Digital Public Library of American (DPLA), for business plans, costs, sustainability, and other aspects related to scale.

I have taken the liberty of extrapolating on membership numbers and financial influence in our survey results in order to speculate on the potential benefits of expanded collaboration among consortia. If the estimated 150 or so consortia that did not respond to our survey were of median size and had a median budget of about $1.2 million, the total aggregate number of libraries involved would exceed 26,000 and the aggregate budget would exceed $349 million. That's a lot of buying power and influence. Granted there is some overlap in membership because some libraries belong to more than one consortium.

Two large consortia, OCLC and LYRASIS, act in some sense as mega-consortia or consortia of consortia. The DPLA has the potential to join them. Might these organizations play an increasingly valuable role in bringing consortia together for more efficiency and enhanced buying power? OCLC has been supporting consortia for years; first, with its primary service of providing access to MARC records, later with an interlibrary loan system, and more recently with discovery and integrated library system services. Consortia have taken advantage of these opportunities with varying levels of participation.

OCLC is a cooperative of librarians, institutions, and organizations worldwide. In 1967 a small group of library leaders believed that if they worked together, they could find solutions to the most pressing issues facing libraries. These leaders began with the idea of combining computer technology with library cooperation to reduce costs and improve services through shared online cataloging. Today as technology has made the world smaller and the reach of libraries greater, OCLC has grown into a worldwide organization in which 23,000 libraries, archives, and museums in 170 countries participate. And the OCLC cooperative is helping libraries define their place in the digital world with new web-scale services that amplify and extend library cooperation even further.

OCLC works through a global network with nearly 600 consortia and groups to connect libraries to manage and share the world's knowledge and to form a community dedicated to the values of librarianship, cooperation, resource sharing, and universal access. OCLC's work with groups varies broadly. It provides group purchasing options for OCLC services such as WorldShare cataloging and interlibrary loan services, virtual reference with QuestionPoint, and resource sharing with VDX. OCLC also provides WebJunction professional development training and training opportunities to member libraries through its Training Partnerships with library consortia.

LYRASIS is a geographically broad consortium. It has the reach, administrative infrastructure, and mission flexibility to work with and across many consortia. LYRASIS acts as the licensing agent for several consortia and works with cooperatives and state library agencies on their licensing agendas and other projects. LYRASIS also works with consortia to coordinate interest and develop interconsortial licenses that benefit multiple organizations with administrative services and group discounts. LYRASIS is active in the open-access community and is working with other organizations to support the movement. For example, LYRASIS is the US agent for SCOAP3 a global project to move high-energy physics journals to an open-access model.

The International Coalition of Library Consortia (ICOLC) has been hosted and supported by LYRASIS for some time. ICOLC facilitates information sharing and networking opportunities at little to no cost to participating consortia. There is no fee for membership or online participation in ICOLC. ICOLC has strong international participation and hosts two annual meetings: one in the United States and one abroad. As an adjunct to ICOLC, LYRAIS also hosts what has become an annual consortial summit meeting. This event includes presentations by participating consortia and conversations about topics of mutual interest.

The Digital Public Library of America (DPLA) launched in April 2013 after a long consensus-building process to create what promises to be America's premier digital library. DPLA was created with substantial grant funding and with wide participation by the library community. It has also provided grant funding to a number of hub institutions and consortia to facilitate the expansion of access to available digital content. DPLA is examining how to remain sustainable and continue to fulfill its mission.

Conclusion

Larger, more efficient consortia are moving forward with important efforts to empower and assist member libraries. The five-state wave of consortia consolidation after the 2008 recession was preceded by a three-state wave in Colorado, Connecticut, and Ohio in 2003–2005, during which 20 regional library systems merged into six. In the past decade 79 library consortia have ceased operations. The latest wave of consolidation could continue to grow as resources are spread thin in a slow-growing economy and as potential efficiencies are realized.

The competition by consortia for state funds is an ongoing challenge. At the national level, LSTA funding from the Institute for Museum and Library Services has been threatened for several years and additional threats are looming.

Two essential priorities for a consortium are local needs and efficiency. Paths to efficiency might include the interconnection of ILSs and web-based access to e-content and resource-sharing services, which would enhance discovery-to-delivery services. The library of the twenty-first century is likely to play a continuously growing role as a community center, be it on an academic campus or in a municipality. The role of consortia in empowering and capacity-building for libraries is strengthened by the growing ability to communicate, meet, and participate in virtual training and consulting services. The need to be located close to members has become less important. That is not to say that the value of a nearby connection to personnel is diminished. Rather, it has simply become unaffordable when other services have a higher priority and technology facilitates virtual people-to-people connections.

Partnerships, multiconsortial efficiency, and outsourcing have great potential to enable consortia to meet member needs more effectively. On the upside, merging consortia has already brought much greater efficiency of scale in some states. On the downside, budget cuts have led to reduction in some services as priorities are reset.

The major challenges facing consortia fall into the following areas:

- sustainability of operations due to decreased public funding or member dues revenue
- effective communications and marketing with a member base that is short-staffed and overly busy
- successful negotiations with vendors that continue to increase pricing or are unable to offer advantageous discounts because of their own business and financial pressures and/or consolidation in the marketplace
- support of large-scale library resource-sharing as libraries transition from traditional physical library materials to e-content
- licensing popular e-book content that will satisfy members' patrons

Opportunities include sharing and partnering on services, such as:

- discounts (wider pools to reduce management/administrative efforts)
- generic resources (including access to shared library policies and job descriptions)
- interstate physical delivery (as interstate discovery improves, use of these traditional materials will decline more slowly)
- licenses (wider pools to reduce management/administrative efforts)
- licenses on emerging content and developing partnerships with vendors
- non-copyright content (including open access and MOOCs)
- shared repositories (physical and electronic)
- technology platforms and development (including open-source)
- virtual training and consulting

Professional activities and networking opportunities for consortial staff and managements are available with the following:

- American Library Association's Association of Specialized and Collaborative Library Agencies (ASCLA)
- International Coalition of Library Consortia (ICOLC)
- LYRASIS

Consortia collaborate on many fronts, and some work in the areas mentioned above is in progress. The Enki e-book platform, described in case studies in this book, is in an early stage of collaboration between several consortia that are attempting to resolve the dilemma of hosting owned e-book content when a commercial host is unsatisfactory or unavailable. Anne Okerson's case study on the wide deal shows a multiconsortial benefit when consortia band together to seek advantageous pricing. Kathy Drozd, at Minitex, describes a successful interstate delivery system with cost-effective, efficient services in four states. Jay Schafer's case study on a shared print project includes multiple consortia taking shared responsibility for housing hard copy of vital scholarly content and freeing up valuable space in libraries in several states for other important purposes.

Several areas deserve further exploration. A chart that outlines the e-content and print spending of every consortium would be enlightening. What is the aggregate spending of more than 200 library consortia's members on library supplies? What if there were only a few online marketplaces for our members to choose from? Aggregating our purchasing power could provide a great deal of clout. One challenge is to maintain competition among vendors.

How will the megaconsortia look in the future? They are already addressing some of our needs. Where could we gain the most from a joint investment? Perhaps the answer is in the vision of Library Renewal with a shared e-book platform and marketplace where librarians strive to develop mutually beneficial relationships with publishers and serve them up for consortia and their members to shop. The technology standards could be developed efficiently, the aggregate use of materials could be measured, and fair pricing models could prevail. Such a project would provide a tremendous benefit to consortia that serve public libraries where ownership of e-books is not assured by existing aggregators.

The next two chapters look at how consortia manage the services offered. Given the financial difficulties found in our study and the key value consortia services offer participating libraries, these chapters help map out a path for sustaining library consortia. While our research suggests times are better for library consortia going into 2015, there is still a great need for library consortia to engage in best practices and excellent customer service.

Southeast Florida Information Network (SEFLIN) Case Study

• •

Author's note: Jeannette Smithee, executive director of the Southeast Florida Information Network (SEFLIN) in Boca Raton, responded thoughtfully and thoroughly to our survey. We asked her if we could use her consortium as an example of the shared consortial experience. We thank her for taking the time and making the effort to work with us to provide follow-up information.

SEFLIN has 36 member libraries, comprised of 25 academic libraries, 9 public libraries, 1 tribal library, and 1 school district. Academic membership includes 2 state universities, 2 state colleges, and 1 large private university, as well as 20 smaller for-profit and nonprofit academic institutions. Public library members include 6 municipal and 3 county systems with 105 branches. The school district has 198 school libraries. There are over 300 library branches included in SEFLIN's membership, which is more than the average of 236 branches for all respondents to our 2012 survey

SEFLIN's 2012–13 budget was about $617,000 after three years of dues and grant reductions. About one-third of its revenue came from member dues and one-third from LSTA grant funding (well below the $2.6 million average). Fees for services contributed about five percent of the budget. Reserve funds were used for about 25 percent of the budget due to the elimination of state funding in 2012–13. SEFLIN's budget was less than half what it was in 2006–07. Income from member dues was lower, due in large part to severe reductions in the member libraries' budgets and fewer grant sources. SEFLIN reduced dues and restructured membership levels to accommodate the reduced fiscal capacity of its members.

In our survey, we asked consortial leaders to describe their most significant current and future challenges, and seven (12%) cited member libraries' financial issues. SEFLIN's response said that its current challenges included membership recruitment and retention, with membership, dues, and governance changes as well as a hope to attract and keep more member libraries. "We are also initiating a legislative advocacy committee to develop a campaign to work on getting state funding restored," said Smithee.

In 2013–14 a significant amount of state funding was restored to allow the annual budget to be increased to about $690,000. In Florida, funding for the regional library systems is not statutory and varies from year-to-year. This restoration will allow SEFLIN to end the use of reserve funds to operate and begin to replenish its resources. Florida state grants to public libraries are also beginning to increase, although prerecession levels have not yet been reached. While many libraries are recovering slowly from the recession, one of the largest public library systems is still experiencing severe financial strain.

The Miami Herald reported on July 16, 2013, that there was a likelihood that the Miami-Dade Public Library System would close nearly half of its 51 branches, with more than 250 layoffs and cutbacks in hours. Further, the mayor announced that he was backing away from an anticipated tax increase to support library services. Dissatisfied commissioners and angry residents prompted him to change his mind, according to the article. Only by concerted efforts from library supporters was a compromise one-year reprieve granted by county commissioners, who agreed to use rainy-day reserves to avoid the massive layoffs for the coming year. The real estate crash in 2008 and its effect on related businesses had a strong effect on the Florida economy and a tax-cutting trend grew in some quarters.

SEFLIN was hit hard by the economic downturn, but it has responded effectively to the challenges, as have many other consortia. The organization was in the process of restructuring information technology services as the recession hit, and logical reductions in force were already lowering staff costs.

SEFLIN's long-term challenge is the same faced by many organizations and businesses, according to Smithee. That challenge is to define, offer, and communicate about new and relevant services for members. "We need more than loyalty now to keep members that constantly have to justify their budgets and activities. We have to push services to member library staff . . . with reduced budgets; library staffs are scheduled tightly and have less time for cooperative committee service and even CE attendance. We need to work at retaining that 'member-connection' with more of our services provided virtually," Smithee wrote.

CHAPTER 3

Managing Consortia

Valerie Horton

> *"Library consortia bring together librarians and libraries for activities and objectives that cannot be as effectively undertaken individually."*
>
> FE ANGELA M. VERZOSA

C onsortia management has never been easy, and the beginning of the twenty-first century has been an especially difficult time for library consortia. As discussed in chapter 2, consortia have been closing, merging, or scaling back services. In response to hard economic times, the remaining consortia have had to become ever more nimble at finding ways of reducing costs, building revenue, and sharing services and collections. All these changes have the benefit of providing greater value to member libraries.

This changing landscape has required consortia managers to expand their knowledge and skills. Managing complex systems with multiple partners requires strong managerial and interpersonal skills as well as expertise in many areas. This chapter provides an overview of consortia governance structures and explores typical management functions. These sections highlight critical aspects of each function and recommend additional resources for further study.

Governance Structures

Most consortia fall into one of five governance structures:

- 501(c)(3) nonprofit organizations
- divisions of a university system(s)
- government organizations (regional or other types of systems supported by state dollars)
- associations
- organizations with no legal status

A manager must understand the organization's governance structure because it can significantly influence which activities are required by law.

501(c)(3) Status

Many consortia are incorporated as 501(c)(3) tax-exempt organizations under the United States Internal Revenue Service (IRS) code. The name refers to Section 501(c) of the *Code of Federal Regulations* that allows certain types of nonprofit organizations to be "exempt" from some federal taxes. Tax-exempt organizations must still pay payroll taxes, and the organization still is required to file a tax return. 501(c)(3) status applies only to federal law. However, many states have chosen to accept the federal status as proof of exemption from state taxation as well.

Compliance with 501(c)(3) status requires that the consortium have articles of incorporation or bylaws that show how the organization's function matches those required of nonprofit organizations. Those functions include providing religious, educational, charitable, scientific, and literary services, to name just a few. Library consortia fall within both the educational and literary service categories. Many well-known library consortia have 501(c)(3) status, including LYRASIS, Amigos Library Services, Midwest Collaborative for Library Services (MCLS), Center for Research Libraries (CRL), OHIONET, WALDO, the Massachusetts Library System, and the Orbis Cascade Alliance.

Tax law does not mandate specific management structures, policies, or practices, but it does require evidence of sound management to comply with audit requirements. State laws can also impact organizational activities and require specific activities or reporting. The following list should be considered a starting point:

1. **Adherence to Stated Purpose:** The organization's purpose is typically found in the articles of incorporation but can also be found in the bylaws. LYRASIS' Articles of Incorporation are: "The corporation was incorporated under Pennsylvania's Nonprofit Corporation Law of 1933, as amended, exclusively for educational and charitable purposes within the meaning of Section 501(c)(3) of the Internal Revenue Code of 1986." This is another example, from the Colorado Library Consortium's (CLiC) bylaws: "Purpose. CLiC fosters and provides leadership and expertise through cooperation and collaboration to improve library service to Colorado residents, and shall have the power to fulfill other educational purposes consistent with Internal Revenue Code §501(c)(3)."

2. **Maintain Records:** Organizations are required to maintain a set of records, typically including the following documents:

   - application form to the IRS for tax-exempt status (Form 1023)
   - IRS letter confirming 501(c)(3) status
   - articles of incorporation, bylaws, and any amendments
   - Tax Identification Number
   - descriptions and summaries of programs
   - minutes from governance meetings
   - employment records, such as W-2 forms
   - financial and tax filing records

   Managers should check for additional state record-retention requirements. Developing financial and employment record-retention policies requires significant expertise. Most states have management support firms that will conduct employment audits to review fiscal and human resources record-retention policies. It is a good idea to undergo an external audit in this area by an expert.

3. **Develop Bylaws:** Bylaws must spell out board membership and the rules for selecting board members must be followed to the letter. If the organization wishes to make changes in board selection or representation, the bylaws must be amended. The board and managers should review the bylaws every few years. Also note, some state laws and regulations impact how governing boards are constituted.

4. **Filing federal tax forms:** Consortia must file federal tax forms such as Form 990, Form-N, or Form 990-EZ. Experienced finance managers will know which forms need to be submitted. If the consortium is too small to have a finance manager, then it is best to work with an accountant who is familiar with nonprofit corporation requirements to ensure that proper forms are filed.

5. **Annual audit:** Sound management practice requires that consortia undergo an annual independent audit. An audit is typically defined as an independent examination of data, statements, records, operations, and financial performances of an organization. Consortia that receive $500,000 or more in a single year in direct or pass-through federal funds must be audited, and there can be state requirements as well. When a consortium receives public funds, specific audit requirements are considered common practice. Recent changes in federal laws, such as the Sarbanes Oxley Act, have increased the complexity and cost of an annual audit, but this is not an area to ignore. An audit demonstrates to the organization's governing board and participating libraries that the manager is following sound fiscal management policy.

6. **State filing:** Many states require a nonprofit to register with the Secretary of State's office every year. Make sure to check your state's specific requirements.

A number of other activities fall under sound management practice, such as following all payroll laws, hiring policies, and employee handbook policies, and having sound budgeting and fiscal procedures in place. These topics will be discussed later in the chapter.

University Governance

A number of consortia have been created under the auspices of a university. Many of these consortia were set up to support resource sharing, digital repositories, remote storage sites, or shared integrated catalog systems across different institutions. Typically these consortia started as academic endeavors, but a number have added services for other types of libraries as well. Examples of consortia that legally exist under university governance are Minitex, GALILEO, Consortia of Academic and Research Libraries in Illinois (CARLI), California Digital Library, the Florida Center for Library Automation, and the Triangle Research Library Network.

Governance under a university structure is both simpler and more complicated than it is for nonprofit organizations. The consortia manager must learn and follow all the bureaucratic rules that govern the university system. Most universities have complex hiring, payroll, legal, auditing, contracting, facilities management, and other systems that benefit the consortia, but they also impose significant constraints and sometimes hefty time and financial burdens.

On the benefit side, the consortium can gain access to specialized experts in areas such as law, contracts, or human resources management at no cost. Physical facilities are often provided at no cost to the cooperative. On the negative side, many academic consortia struggle to follow inflexible, externally imposed rules, and in some cases even the consortium's mission and vision can be limited by university dictates. At the worst, these constraints can impede innovation and flexibility, particularly in the area of human resources and contracting. For instance, it is not uncommon for a university to have multiple personnel classifications systems (e.g., union, faculty, civil service, professional, and administrative) that may or may not match the personnel needs of the consortia. Other services such as utilities, security, facilities management, and technology infrastructure are often much easier for the consortia to adapt to and are much less expensive than for a stand-alone organization.

Typically, under university governance, the manager reports to a university dean. However, a manager may have other bosses, such as the state's office of higher education or an oversight board made up of participating libraries. University personnel can have an academic view of the library world that works well for academic-only cooperatives but may make it difficult for managing services to public, school, and special libraries. Under this governance structure, it is the manager's duty to make the views of the wider library audience known to the university culture. Overall the benefits of access to university intellectual capital, facilities, technology, and services far outweigh any complexities and constraints inherent in adherence to bureaucratic university structures.

Governmental Entities

A number of consortia exist under state governance structures. Many of these consortia are connected to state libraries, and in some cases they are the state library agency acting like a consortium. In other states, regional library systems are created by state law and are separate from the state library. These regional systems are often subdivided by geographic area or type of library served. Examples of these types of consortia include Tex-Share, OhioLINK, Keystone Library Network, and Florida Virtual Campus. Examples of regional systems include Reaching Across Illinois Library System (RAILS), Northeast Kansas Library System (NEKLS), and the Viking Library System in Minnesota.

Consortia that fall under state libraries are likely to be governed by state regulations, law, and restrictions. These consortia must follow state procurement, personnel, and contracting rules and regulations, which can add complexity to the manager's job in much the same way that it does for consortia under university governance. However, working within state systems can become overwhelmingly cumbersome and may not be balanced by as many benefits found in university bureaucracies. It is not uncommon to hear a state library manager complain about spending substantial amounts of time finding "workarounds" of restrictive state rules and regulations to accomplish critical tasks. It is a shame that so much creativity that could be spent providing innovative services to participating libraries is instead spent working around bureaucratic limits.

As mentioned before, a variant of the governmental structures are regional library systems. Regional systems became popular in the 1970s and 1980s. They were created to support local libraries services by jointly funding activities such as integrated library systems, resource sharing, delivery, and continuing education. A number of states enacted regional library systems laws to expand public library service to underserved rural areas.

Regional systems are divided by geography or by the type of library served, such as public, school, academic, or multitype systems. In New York, for example, regional systems were developed for public, school, and academic systems as well as nine multitype regional councils. In most states, however, regional systems are geared to public libraries or serve multitype libraries. Some regional systems have close ties to the state library; others are only loosely affiliated, depending on the state's regional library law. A number of regional systems are all but independent from the state and may have 501(c)(3) status. Many states, such as Rhode Island, Utah, New Mexico, and Hawaii, never developed regional systems.

As stated in chapter 2, regional library systems have been particularly hard hit recently with five states collapsing multiple regional systems. Other regional systems, such as those in California and Florida, are struggling. However, regional library systems in many states, such as those in Kansas, Minnesota, and Nebraska, are still doing well.

No Legal Status

While no statistics exist on the number of unaffiliated consortia, it is likely that they are common, both forming and closing with great frequency. In many cases these entities come together for a single purpose, such as hosting a one-time event, sharing a single cooperative purchase, working on specific project, or developing library advocacy materials. These groups may exist for just a short period of time or continue for decades. In Colorado, for instance, an unaffiliated group of libraries has been hosting an interlibrary loan conference for over 44 years. This group has never felt a need to incorporate, although it recently created a fiscal relationship with a consortium. Another example is the Digital Commonwealth in Massachusetts, which has operated since 2007 without a corporate structure. However, it has recently decided to seek not-for-profit corporate status. Groups without legal status often become the genesis of new consortia. As the group matures or the projects take on more fiscal or organizational impact, there is a logical need to create a legal structure to manage the relationship. The economics of cooperation suggest that the trend of libraries joining together in group projects will continue and possibly even accelerate. These groups are exploring creative ways of obtaining sustainable funding as public funding becomes more difficult to get. It is safe to assume that more groups without legal status will continue to form for the foreseeable future, perhaps prompting the rebirth of the library consortia movement.

Management Practices

The next section deals with the main activities, such as planning, hiring, and budgeting, in which a manager engages on a day-to-day basis. But before we explore these areas, it is worthwhile to ask what skills a manager should have. Obviously a manager has to have a significant knowledge of both library science and management functions as well as strong leadership skills. A manager also should be able to analyze complex organizations and follow significant trends at a regional, state, national, and even international level. In many cases consortia managers are drawn from the ranks of experienced library managers, who bring a strong background in library service into the cooperative.

Along with the ability to see the big picture, a manager must be able to visualize different approaches to the current situation and ask appropriate questions. These are the kinds of questions a manager should ask:

- Will a reorganization help improve the organization?
- Will a new technology improve efficiency?
- Are employee resources appropriately assigned or are staff adequately trained?
- What functions should the manager engage in and what should be delegated?

A manager must have the political and interpersonal skills to navigate many complex relationships with stakeholders, library leaders, and other library organizations in the area. The ability to listen, cooperate, and delegate as well as to lead is essential. More on this complex topic is provided in chapter 5.

The next section deals with most major day-to-day operations that take place in a typical consortium, starting with the key issues of budgeting and human resources.

Budgeting and Financial Management

Budgeting tends to be a struggle for managers. All library budgets are complex, but consortia budgets tend to have additional layers of complexity. Minitex gives an example of this complexity. Its funding and support services come from numerous entities, including the Minnesota Office of Higher Education, the University of Minnesota, the Minnesota Historical Society via legislative appropriations, and from federal grants such as those from the Library Services and Technology Act (LSTA), from other grant sources, from cooperative ventures with other consortium, contractually from North Dakota and South Dakota, and from fees charged to libraries for using specific services or products. All of these funding sources have requirements or strings attached. At the minimum, funds must be spent matching the funder's requirements, reports must be filed, and communication channels to funders and to recipients of the services must be maintained.

A consortium's budget and financial reports must clearly show how funds were received and how the expenditures match the requirements from the funding source. But often any given consortial service may be funded by numerous entities (i.e., the four different funders who support Minitex's resource-sharing network). If there is a financial change with one funding source, it can directly impact the services offered to others. Managing and tracking this complex set of interrelations is both time consuming and difficult. Truly, managing different interests can be one of the most difficult tasks a manager may face.

Most consortia run some form of accounting or financial management system. These financial systems may be small systems run on software such as Excel, QuickBooks, or Peachtree, or they may be part of very large institutional systems like PeopleSoft, Lawson Software, or Oracle. Basically, financial management systems help with reports, fiscal queries, and budgets. All invoices and payments are recorded in these systems, so they give the manager and governing board an objective, big-picture overview of the financial assets of the consortium while at the same time providing detailed reports on every invoice handled. Another major reason to use a financial management system is that it allows for internal controls that separate tasks to minimize the risk of fiscal irregularities while allowing accountants or auditors to interact with financial data in an efficient manner.

In addition to financial management systems, many consortium managers have found it advisable to engage outside firms to handle payroll. Payroll laws and taxing structures are complex and change frequently, and even large organizations outsource payroll. Many payroll companies have well-developed, online interfaces for managing employee payroll and benefits that can be a real benefit to both managers and employees. These firms tend to charge reasonable fees while helping to eliminate costly errors, and they reassure governance entities that proper care of fiscal resources is being taken.

Learning how to budget often happens as part of on-the-job-training when a new manager is hired. Many managers spend their initial weeks on a new job trying to understand the thinking of the person who previously held that position. Library schools do provide an introduction to budgeting but do not offer the advanced training needed to manage a cooperative. For more information on financial issues, managers can go to library sources or to the nonprofit sector. ALA has a nice selection of resources on its Budgeting and Finance page at www.ala.org/tools/atoz/librarybudgetfinance/budgetfinance. The best budgeting resources tend to come from the nonprofit sector. Consider: *The Budget-Building Book for Nonprofits: a Step-by-Step Guide for Managers and Boards*.

Although it is fee-based, one of the best sources for information on anything in the nonprofit sector, including budgeting, is BoardSource (https://boardsource.org/eWeb/). BoardSource has a number of high-quality, free publications, such as *Board Basics 101*, *Fiduciary Responsibilities*, *Legal and Compliance Issues*, and *Nonprofit Governance and the Sarbanes-Oxley Act*. Many cities have organizations dedicated to supporting nonprofits, which can be found through the Council of Nonprofits (www.councilofnonprofits.org). These councils are a great place to find classes and webinars, and also to meet others who wish to learn more about budgeting.

The best advice for managers who are starting a new job is to get to know your staff on day one and to learn your budget on day two. The more you understand how finances work in your consortium, the better you will be able to handle the rest of the management issues listed in this section.

Human Resources

Human resource (HR) management is another difficult and challenging part of consortia management. There is an abundance of employment and labor laws, regulations, and common practices related to managing the workforce of an organization. HR is responsible for hiring, firing, paying, training, promoting, providing benefits, and assessing employees. HR also has oversight of labor relations for larger shops with unions, succession planning, harassment issues, diversity, and employee handbooks, and it deals with an endless array of people-related issues and problems. When a problem arises, any of the topics listed above can suddenly become the biggest time-sink for a consortium director. Pending personnel lawsuits can feel like the sword of Damocles.

It is beyond the scope of this book to go into every human resource issue. However, there are several things a consortium manager can do to make management in this area more efficient and less problem-focused:

1. Have a good accountant or fiscal manager who can file or oversee the filing of all appropriate employment-related forms, such as employment eligibility verification and the tax forms for independent contractors.
2. Retain a lawyer who specializes in government or not-for-profit legal issues to answer questions.
3. Find a management company that specializes in employment practice. These companies provide invaluable advice about hiring, firing, assessing, and promoting employees as well as employee benefits and handbook creation. They often have rich websites that provide many templates needed to create policies and guidelines.
4. Prepare an employee handbook and update it at least every two years.
5. Attend webinars, workshops, and conference programs that have HR programming.

An interesting new trend is that some libraries are starting to share or consolidate library staff using the consortium as the consolidator of services. For instance, the Triangle Research Library Network (TRLN) is working on a collaborative staffing model that will support staff development, allow sharing of expertise and specialized skills, and facilitate the distribution of workloads and the sharing of positions. "Activities may include the creation of internships or fellowships within TRLN libraries, and the exploration of job trading and sharing," according to their website. The Orbis Cascade Alliance is building a joint technical services staff to support their new shared catalog. Working out HR relationships in a collaborative will be a unique challenge.

Another interesting trend is a library consortium serving as a temporary agency for member libraries. The Massachusetts Library System service is an example. The system provides skilled library staff to fill in for vacancies that occur in participating libraries much like a regular temp agency does. For more information, see the BiblioTemps case study.

These new HR trends are worth watching as they may provide a way of maximizing limited fiscal resources.

Planning and Assessment

Strategic planning is the process by which an organization defines its place in the larger library context. When an organization plans, it discusses its future aspirations and develops goals, making detailed action plans to achieve those goals. Through the planning process, staff and stakeholders figure out where the organization currently is and where it is going. Michael Wilkinson, the creator of the Driver Planning Model, states there are five primary reasons to plan:

1. To set direction and priorities
2. To get everyone on the same page
3. To simplify decision-making
4. To drive alignment (arranging resources to maximize strategic success)
5. To communicate the message

Assessment is included in this section because it helps to determine the most critical items to measure. Many libraries and consortia have been taking measures based on past practice rather than as a means to evaluate the quality of current functions or to better gauge which new functions should be undertaken. It is important to routinely ask stakeholders for their perceptions of the consortium's services. It is also important to include the staff in any assessment or planning activities. Staff have their fingers on the members' pulse, and their buy-in is essential to the success of any plan.

There are many well-known planning methods. *The Executive Guide to Facilitating Strategy* by Michael Wilkinson provides step-by-step guidance. *Strategic Planning and Management for Library Managers*, by Joseph R. Matthews, has been around for many years. *Strategic Planning for Results* by Sandra Nelson has been used extensively in public libraries. More recently, the Edge Initiative has been gaining popularity in public libraries. The Edge's website says it "...is a voluntary assessment program that provides libraries with benchmarks, best practices, tools, and resources that support continuous improvement and reinvestment in public technology services. Edge helps libraries connect their services to community priorities." For academics, there is "Strategic Planning in College Libraries," a *CLIP Note* that outlines the planning process used in twenty-five academic libraries of all sizes. There are also a number of books geared towards nonprofit planning, such as David La Piana's *The Nonprofit Strategies Revolution* or John M. Bryson's *Strategic Planning for Public and Nonprofit Organizations*.

Advocacy and Public Relations

Federal and state laws dictate whether consortia staff can advocate. In general, organizations that receive public funds are restricted in their ability to do advocacy work. Restrictions tend to be strongest on government agencies and universities. Lobbying restrictions include using work-time or work equipment (phones, copier, e-mail, etc.), posting signs, and wearing campaign items. Further, most employees of public entities are prohibited from any kind of campaigning or lobbying with elected officials. Some states do allow limited gifts to elected officials, for example, fifty dollars a year to pay for an occasional lunch. Organizations are expected to track all expenditures on elected officials. Regulations vary in each state.

Many consortia employees are members of library associations, and through these associations use their dues, personal contributions, and nonwork time to advocate in support of libraries. In some states, nonprofit employees can lobby but must track all expenses by legislator. It may be wise for a manager to show up at library advocacy events on nonwork time, even if he or she cannot speak in an official capacity. Showing up goes a long way toward building support with stakeholders. One of the best sources of library advocacy is the ALA's website *Advocacy University* (www.ala.org/advocacy/advocacy-university). Also consider using ALA's *Library Advocate's Handbook*, which is available for download from the ALA website at a low cost.

While advocacy must be carefully monitored, consortia staff has much more leeway when it comes to marketing. Consortia can and should create campaigns that support the use of library services. In many states the state library takes the lead in marketing, with consortia supporting the campaign. Wyoming has done several humorous and impactful campaigns geared towards the general public. The star of the Wyoming campaign, mud-flap girl, has gained minor celebrity and a bit of notoriety—a sign of a successful campaign.

When developing a marketing campaign, the first question to ask is to whom are you marketing. Is your audience the staff from participating member libraries, the general public, the academic community, or some other entity? This question can be surprisingly difficult to answer. In most library consortia, there are different opinions about whether to market the consortium itself or to market the organization's service directly to library patrons. Is the goal to make the consortium more visible to members and potential members? Or is the goal to promote a particular service that patrons use? What about raising the organization's profile with legislators? The lines can easily get blurred. Having these questions answered at the beginning of your project can save a lot time later. It is possible that managers may want to market to consortia members and to the general public and to legislators. In that case, it may be best to have a unique campaign for each audience.

Public Relations campaigns that target library staff are geared towards convincing participant libraries that being a member of the consortia is in their best interest and that individual consortial services can benefit their library patrons. These campaigns frequently feature key consortium services with the goal of getting new libraries to sign up for the product or existing libraries to remain in a specific service. Below is a graphic featuring the Lynx logo used to encourage libraries to join Colorado's shared statewide databases. The colors on the website are deep blue and black; check it out at www.librarylynx.org.

Consortia websites are a major marketing tool providing access to both products and services offered. Consortia websites often have the same problem as library websites: in general, too much information is shoved into too small a place. That said, the website is the primary marketing tool

for most organizations and deserves considerable attention from the manager. It can be difficult to find information on creating a quality website for a consortium. However, there are good books and blogs on designing a library website, such as J. Poolos' *Designing, Building, and Maintaining Web Sites*. Overall, studying other consortia websites may be the best options.

Communication

Consortia managers often say that communication is a major source of frustration. It seems no matter how often a manager sends out e-mail, places a message on a website or blog, writes up a newsletter piece, posts on social media, makes an announcement at a conference, or calls a librarian directly, member libraries still will say that they never saw or heard the information. There is a truism in communication theory: by the time you're sick and tired of repeating yourself, you're just beginning to be heard.

Communication is about sending clear, focused information about the consortium's plans, services, or political situation. A manager must constantly communicate, use different communication channels, and repeat the message. People hear a message when they are ready to hear it, and nothing will change that. However there are some things that make communication work better. People tend to listen to messages from someone they know personally. Personal connections help word-of-mouth communication spread, so have different people send out messages even on the same topics. The more consortium staff interacts with participating library staff, the better chance there is of being heard.

Remember that different people prefer different communication media. Use print, blogs, social media, videos, phone calls, bookmarks, postcards, magnets, flyers, meeting announcements, webinars, and conference workshops to send key messages. For some messages, humor or clever graphics can be effective. If appropriate, putting a catchy or humorous headline on the message may increase notice, but be careful not to go over-the-top, as that may alienate part of the organization's constituency. Attention spans are short and library employees are busy, so a shorter message often will be heard over a longer one. In fact, several consortia have recently polled members on communication preferences, and the short e-mail message is ranked the number-one preference. Finally, there is no reason to explain everything about your organization's program, policy, or decision. Stick with the highlights and offer links to more complete information for those who are interested. Remember: short, impactful messages have a better chance of being heard.

Senior managers must keep in mind that people want to hear from those at the top of the organization, especially about major policy changes or new strategic directions. The head of the consortium is a critical voice in reaching out to library staff, library leaders, and stakeholders. Remember also to tell people the "why" of a decision, not just the "what" and "how." If you don't convince most people about the "why" of a coming change, those people are likely to make up their own minds about why. Simon Sinek's *Start with Why* is a great resource for crafting impactful messages.

Literature on library communication theory deals mainly with outreach to patrons, though much of that information is pertinent to management communication as well. Consider consulting an older but valuable title, *Library Public Relations, Promotions and Communications* by Lisa A. Wolfe. General management literature is overflowing with information on communication. Two excellent sources are *The Voice of Authority* by Dianna Booher and *Shut Up and Say Something* by Karen Friedman.

Conclusion

Overall, consortia management looks a lot like library management. These similarities are one of the reasons so many new consortia managers come from participating libraries. However, there are unique features of consortia management that make the task different from and sometimes more complex than running a single library. Governance structure significantly impacts the authority and responsibilities of a consortia manager. Governance structures can place severe limits on an organization and impact the type of services offered. A university-owned consortium may well focus on creating resource-sharing networks and cooperative purchases of databases. A regional multitype consortium may focus on providing databases and offering wide-ranging training options. The needs of participating libraries drive these decisions.

Regardless of governance structure, consortia managers always must be considering the needs and requirements of diverse sets of participating libraries. At other times, different needs of participating members can cause conflict as the consortia manager attempts to navigate complex relationships. The manager must be able to sort through all these levels and present a clear vision of what is doable and what is wise to do. No small task!

CHAPTER 4

Consortia Services

Valerie Horton

T he previous chapter dealt with standard management issues that are common in libraries, businesses, and nonprofit organizations alike. Consortia managers perform many activities that are unique. These special services are offered to participating libraries and are often the main reason the consortium exists. As stated in chapter 2, the six services most commonly offered according to a number of consortia surveys were training, shared electronic content, group purchasing, physical delivery, consulting, and shared integrated library system (ILS). This chapter goes into detail about these six functions as well as others such as digital libraries and institutional repository functions. More on these topics can be found in the case studies section. The purpose of this chapter and the case studies is to provide a clear picture of the current activities of library consortia as well as to allow existing consortia to compare their services against consortia norms and learn about potential new services to offer participating libraries.

Cataloging

In 1976 about 15 percent of consortia reported providing cataloging services to members.[1] By 2007 a large nationwide consortia study did not even ask about cataloging. In our 2012 study, only two consortia reported doing contract cataloging. While these studies suggest that many consortia no longer offer professional cataloging services, there are still some cases where cataloging support has great value. This is particularly the case for consortia with union catalogs where there is a strong desire to have quality bibliographic records in the system or for larger consortia that offer it as a pay-for-service to members upon request. The pay-for-service model includes retrospective cataloging, ongoing current cataloging, and special projects such as assistance with metadata creation or switching to Resource Description and Access (RDA) or the Library of Congress's Bibliographic Framework Initiative (BibFrame).

Consulting

Consultant have a broad mandate that includes everything from weeding collections to new building design to handling book challenges to technology training. Consultants in consortia are trainers and event organizers, and they may also work virtual reference shifts. These employees are often on the road at participating libraries or at other library events. Consultants need to have a wide variety of library experiences and a passion for learning because much of what they do is learned on the job. To the wider library community, the consultant is an important personal connection back to the consortium.

Consultants are asked to address a broad range of issues—basically any issue in any library that may come up. It is not uncommon for consultants to specialize in specific areas such as supervision, technical services, school librarianship, or technology. Managers should tell these employees not to fake knowledge if they don't know a subject area. It is far better to learn what they need or provide a referral to someone else who can help with a particular problem. In this author's opinion, it is better not to allow consultants to become involved in a given library's human resource problem or board conflict. In situations in which lawsuits are likely, it is best to refer to professional ombudsmen, lawyers, or organizations that specialize in human resource management. State library staff also can be good sources for legal help.

Like continuing education professionals, consultants tend to be fiscal loss leaders. Since consultants tend to be professional librarians, salaries can be high. Consultants need substantial travel budgets, mobile communication technology, and time and resources for personal skills development. In times of retrenchment, consultants, like trainers, are often the first to be laid off. However, these layoffs come at a high price. Without employees dedicated to the outreach function, a consortium can become isolated from member libraries. Rehiring these employees is recommended as soon as funding becomes available.

Continuing Education and Training

Continuing education has been a bedrock service of consortia for a long time. Continuing education events can cover multiple topic areas or a specific service function such as metadata creation. Conferences typically cover multiple topics; for instance, a conference might cover patron privacy, the reference interview, RDA record creation, and trends in customer service. Training is often related to the key services of the organization, such as support for a shared e-book system or appropriate use of a delivery service.

Training staff are typically professional librarians who are often technologically savvy or have extensive professional expertise. Trainers need the best communication and presentation equipment that the organization can afford, as well as access to resources to develop their own skills as a trainer. The best trainers tend to be engaging, creative, and experimental in providing information to member libraries. There are a number of organizations that support library trainers, such as ALA's LEARN Round Table. Becoming a trainer is a great way to learn the skills that are critical in the profession and can be a stepping stone to advancement.

Continuing education rarely makes any revenue for consortia. Training is far more likely to be subsidized by the organization than to be a secure revenue source. The costs to support training activities are quite high, and unfortunately, the library marketplace cannot handle high registration fees. A quality training course, if developed internally, can easily take a week or more to create. Paying outside trainers to offer courses can easily cost thousands of dollars a day. Plus there are the costs of marketing, technology, facilities, training materials, travel and accommodations, and refreshments.

Online training has become popular to reduce travel costs for both trainers and attendees and achieve greater geographic penetration. Most library consortia offer webinars. In fact there are so many webinars offered these days that training events may start losing value for attendees. Blended learning training includes a combination of in-person, online, and self-paced training. Short training videos are popular but require expertise to develop and can be difficult to keep current. The same is true for self-paced tutorials. Most training surveys find that respondents want a range of different training methods offered. Providing multiple training methods can add complexity and cost but also is most likely to meet the needs of the widest variety of participants.

In organizations that are retrenching, continuing education is one of the first items cut. Unfortunately cutting training, like cutting consultants, can create a negative spiral. There are always new people coming into member libraries that need to be trained to keep up the quality level. Nonexistent or inadequate training programs have a direct impact on the consortium's perceived value by member libraries. Balancing the costs versus the need for staff training is difficult, but it is also a critical function for the library consortia manager. To learn more about continuing education, consider *Staff Development: A Practical Guide*, edited by Andrea Wigbels Stewart, et al., or *Workplace Learning & Leadership: A Handbook for Library and Nonprofit Trainers* by Lori Reed and Paul Signorelli.

Cooperative Collection Development

Cooperative collection development (CCD) can be defined as two or more libraries coordinating or sharing the development of a materials collection. Historically many academic consortia have attempted to create CCD models. Many of these early attempts were journal-based and had only limited long-term viability. Perception of local needs and leadership changes often derailed early attempts at building collaborative collections.

Today, with so many shared ILSs, sophisticated physical delivery systems, and electronic and digital resources, there has been a significant expansion in CCD. A study done by cooperating libraries in 2010 found that they were able to "provide compelling evidence for the value of collaborative purchasing to library administrators and university officials."[2]

The California Digital Library's Shared Print Collection aims to "further optimize the management of information resources for students and faculty by reducing unnecessary duplication, leveraging shared assets ..., and expanding the information resources available system-wide, while meeting the information needs of library users at each campus," according to its website. However, the real action in cooperative collection development is with electronic resources. Many academic libraries are participating in multiple e-resource collections through different consortia projects. Many of these services are now doing demand-drive acquisitions, which allows patrons to help build e-collections.

CCD has also expanded into the public library marketplace. States like Wisconsin, Colorado, and Kansas offer shared e-book collections for public libraries. These collections of popular materials are particularly beneficial to small and medium-sized libraries who gain more buying power for their limited resources. Libraries contribute to these collections through acquisition formulas that are often based on a population served, though some states use federal or state funding to build these collections. The major criticism of these collections is availability for high-demand titles. Typically there is a formula to buy more copies of popular titles; for instance, for every five patron hold requests, a new e-book is purchased. However, it can be still difficult to buy enough of any given title during its initial popular surge.

E-resources are driving a renewed interest in cooperative collection development that is likely to continue to grow. In fact, e-books can become the foundation for new cooperative ventures that use shared collections as a stepping-stone to greater cooperation between participating libraries. CCD and demand-driven acquisition is changing so rapidly that journal literature or blog posts remain the best way of learning more about this topic.

Cooperative Purchasing

Cooperative purchasing is a complex and vital part of many consortia. In fact, many consortia started as cooperative purchasing ventures and later expanded to other services. The economics are clear: the more libraries joining a cooperative purchase, the more leverage negotiators have to reach better deals. Databases and e-resource packages make up the bulk of cooperative purchases; there are hundreds of databases available in the marketplace. A number of consortia arrange for discounts on purchasing furniture, technology, and supplies. Some consortia go further and serve as technology support for member libraries. In this case, the consortium owns and maintains electronic equipment that is placed in participating libraries.

A typical library may purchase from multiple consortia. According to The Medical University of South Carolina Library's website, it purchases from the following organizations: National Network of Libraries of

Medicine, LYRASIS, Southeastern Atlantic Regional Medical Library Service, Consortium of Southern Biomedical Science Libraries, Digital Information for South Carolina Users, PASCAL, Library Director's Forum of the South Carolina Commission of Higher Education, Science Direct Project, Charleston Academic Library Consortium, Fort Johnson Cooperative Agreement, Bioengineering Program with Clemson University, and AHEC Information Services. For a large library, purchasing from 13 consortia is not unusual, and even small public libraries typically have access to databases from more than one source.

Much has been written on the big deal database purchases. With big deals consortia negotiate multimillion dollar packages for hundreds, if not thousands, of scholarly titles. While there is some dissatisfaction with the contents of these packages, the savings are often substantial. Lately, some organizations have created wide deals. In this scenario, several consortia join together to negotiate the deal, creating even larger purchasing blocks (see Case Study 5, Embracing Wide Deals). The growing trend toward open-access titles may start changing the publishing landscape, but for the foreseeable future it is likely that many consortia will continue to negotiate the big deals for member libraries.

Consortia also provide many niche databases on everything from auto repair to genealogy to health care to learning a language. Typically, the consortium takes a small percentage off the discount from vendors as a fee for service. Some consortia also charge membership fees tied to participating in cooperative purchases. For others cooperative purchasing revenue is the main income source. Depending on cooperative purchasing revenue can be problematic, as there is more competition in this marketplace, especially among academic libraries. In addition some vendors appear to be tightening discount schemes, making the margin of revenue even smaller. Diversifying funding sources should be a major effort of any manager who finds cooperative purchasing to be the main revenue source for her organization.

Digitization Services

A digital library is a collection of objects stored in digital format. Typically this content includes photos, posters, newspapers, audio files, letters, maps, oral histories, historic documents, reports, postcards, yearbooks, diaries, books, and more. These objects come not just from library collections but also from cultural heritage institutions such as museums, archives, historical societies, and art museums. Many are primary source materials.

HathiTrust, Europeana, Internet Archives, and the Digital Public Library of American (DPLA) are all large digital libraries. Some of these digital libraries hold the digital objects; others provide searching of metadata that links to the home location of the digital object. For example, DPLA aggregates the metadata from a growing number of regional digital catalogs. DPLA also includes exhibits from an expanding list of hubs including the Digital Commonwealth of Massachusetts, Kentucky Digital Library, and the Mountain West Digital Library, among others. DPLA also aggregates content hubs, which contain access to vast collections from the Smithsonian, New York Public Library, Harvard University, the National Archives, and HathiTrust.

Many consortia or regions are also building cooperative digital catalogs; at this writing at least 30 states have some kind of digital library. Many of these libraries were built upon digitized collections of historic photographs or newspapers. Some states have been lucky enough to get state funding to build historical digital collections; others have depended on grant funding. It makes sense to collaborate on digital services given the expertise required to develop and use format requirements such as metadata standards. Expertise is also required to know digital scanning technologies and to organize and display digital objects in a patron-accessible manner. Outreach, training, and marketing are typically included in consortia services that support digital libraries.

New trends in digital libraries include building exhibits, preservation of digital objects, and opening collections to patron-developed applications. Many digital libraries are reaching out to the user community, soliciting comments on digital objects held in their collection as well as actually collecting personal histories or stories from patrons. The future of these digital consortia is uncertain because sustainable funding is not uncertain.

ALA's Association of Specialized and Collaborative Library Agencies (ASCLA) Collaborative Digitization Interest Group members have helped pioneer many of the metadata and digitization standards that are now norms, and the group is worth joining. There are a number of books on digitization, including Anna E. Bulow and Jess Ahmon's *Preparing Collections for Digitization*, Diane Kresh's *The Whole Digital Library Handbook*, and Allison Zhang and Don Gourley's *Creating Digital Collections: A Practical Guide*.

Institutional Repositories and the Library as Publisher

Institutional repositories (IR) are digital collections that house, preserve, and disseminate the intellectual output of a research institution. IRs typically include faculty research papers, preprints, theses and dissertations, datasets, documents, and other objects of importance to an institution. Some institutions use the IR as a source for displaying special collections materials including image, audio, and video files. Many institutions place copies of their own policies, contracts, minutes, newsletters, and reports in the repository. IRs can also be used to store teaching resources, serving as a place for students to find faculty-generated materials such as course notes, and a space for student projects or student organizations.

IRs are often valued as a method of providing cost-controlled access to scholarly materials, or as some would say, to wrestle monopoly control from for-profit publishers and high-fee scholarly societies. But repositories also help to expand research awareness by showcasing all of an institution's scientific, social, and achievements in one place. An IR allows a library to facilitate development of a research institution's intellectual property while retaining the publication rights to the author's work.

Several consortia have attempted to leverage the price of building and maintaining an IR by hosting it centrally, while others allow each participating institution to customize the IR to their own needs. The Colorado Alliance of Research Libraries hosts seven institutions, including one public library, in their repository. The Alliance's website states, "Our purpose is to help member institutions preserve and provide access to digital assets of enduring value that are critical to their work in research, education, and cultural heritage." The Alliances' list of services includes training, documentation, best practice guidelines, technical support, and metadata preparation assistance. The California Digital Library's (CDL) IR website states its goal is to "manage, archive, and share its valuable digital content." CDL focuses on the ease of placing items in the IR, the value of sharing the information with others, the IR's ability to meet data sharing and preservation requirements of grant-funded projects, and on the long-term preservation of the valuable and unique collections.

IR services are specialized and are often limited to academic consortia, although there were some early attempts to use IR systems to collect local community-generated materials. For more information on this topic, read Md. Zahid Hossain Shoeb's *Institutional Repository Planning and Implementation: Strategic and Technical Issues*, or Jonathan A. Nabe's *Starting, Strengthening, and Managing Institutional Repositories*.

Libraries and consortia have been slow to jump on the "library as publisher" bandwagon. The Library Publishing Coalition claims over 55 percent of academic libraries are developing or offering publishing services. Both public and academic libraries are teaching patrons how to publish online, often using open-access publishing software. Public libraries also have a long history of publishing local print monographs or shorter chapbooks of interest to their communities. What's new is that a few of these libraries are now using print-on-demand equipment like the Espresso Book Machine to print patron monographs. In a few cases, consortia support publishing in libraries by providing training, Espresso machines, or access to software systems. The Douglas County Library System (CO) has created a model for hosting locally created content that is gaining the attention of consortia. Several consortia, such as CALIFA, MARMOT, Amigos Library Services, NC LIVE, and the State of Kansas, are experimenting with similar platforms.

While still few in number, some library consortia are becoming publishers. Several library science journals are managed by consortia or associations. *Collaborative Librarianship*, for instance, is supported by two Colorado consortia. SUNY's Geneseo is publishing 15 open-access textbooks a year with librarians serving as editors. (See Case Study 6, Open SUNY Textbook Program.) To track trends in academic publishing check out the Library Publishing Coalition, self-described as a community-driven initiative to advance library publishing.

Integrated Library Systems

Most shared ILSs are run by consortia, and ILS support is one of the more common reasons for the creation of new library consortia. Libraries are choosing to join cooperatives to lower costs or spread costs out among many libraries, to end in-house hardware maintenance, to join resource-sharing systems, and to gain the advantage of deeper collaboration with nearby libraries. Marshall Breeding, in his 2011 annual review of the automation marketplace in *Library Journal*, predicted that a growing number of libraries would choose to join shared systems in states without a mandated regional ILS system. In Colorado, prior to 2009, 34 percent of public libraries were using either a shared catalog or sharing in a catalog that consolidated separate holdings into a large union catalog (e.g., MARMOT, Prospector). By 2013, that number had grown to over 65 percent of public libraries.

There are four primary types of cooperative arrangements for shared catalogs:

1. **Separate systems:** In this model a consortium maintains multiple copies of a catalog system, and each participating library has their own use of the software. This model ensures the highest level of autonomy but still provides some cost sharing. The drawback with this model is that it is difficult to allow easy patron-centered resource sharing. WALDO is an example of this model, running an academic version of Koha for libraries in the Northeast.

2. **Separate systems linked into a union catalog:** In this model each library maintains an integrated library system, but the data is harvested on a regular basis and added to a union catalog, which allows for resource sharing. Examples of this model include Prospector, Contra Costa, and OhioLINK.

3. **Union catalog (members retain item ownership):** All members add records to one union catalog, attaching their holdings data to a single bibliographic record shared by the cooperative. Ownership of the individual item remains with the originating library. There are many examples of this model, including PINES, MnPALS, and AspenCat.

4. **Union catalog (shared item ownership):** A new trend is for library e-collections to be shared by the collaborative, instead of residing with the originating libraries.

For consortia, an ILS is a popular and important service that requires significant staffing. Skilled staff is required to support the software, network, and hardware. As a result, a number of consortia are moving toward purchasing network and hardware support from remote vendor sites. Typically, libraries participating in a shared ILS are provided with technical assistance, troubleshooting, and training by the cooperative. Membership committees are used to build guidelines, policies, and best practices.

Pricing is always an issue within cooperative ILSs. Whether an ILS is run by a library or by a consortium, these systems remain expensive. Historically library venders have not offered a significant price break for cooperating libraries. As a result many consortia have moved to open-access systems such as Koha, Evergreen, or the new Kuali OLE. No matter what type of system is selected, convincing members that they must pay an adequate amount to maintain a high-quality system and support for that service can be a challenge.

Physical Delivery

An OCLC report explains that "end users generally don't see the point of finding things they can't get." This point can be missed by library staff focusing on creating patron discovery systems.[3] The report asserted that, "the end user's experience of the delivery of a wanted item is as important, if not more important, than his or her discovery experience." Delivery is a critical piece of the resource-sharing cycle that we refer to as discovery to delivery.

Many consortia provide physical delivery services. A 2008 survey found that 30 states had delivery services, and "anecdotal evidence suggests that almost all of the lower forty-eight states have one or more couriers in operation within their state boundaries."[4] Almost every major public or academic library system has an internal delivery service. In many cases these systems connect to other consortia-run delivery services, creating a hub-and-spoke network. Some cooperative delivery services are limited to a specific city or set of academic libraries; others provide statewide service, and a few systems cross state lines, such as the long-standing delivery network that includes Minnesota, Wisconsin, and the Dakotas (see Case Study 7, Interstate Library Delivery). Delivery drivers visit area libraries, and they may be the representative of the consortium that is seen most frequently. The courier driver becomes the face for the organization, which can be problematic because many consortia outsource delivery to commercial vendors.

Some academic systems need rapid delivery and use more expensive services such as United Parcel Service (UPS) or Federal Express (FedEx). Surprisingly some consortia don't provide delivery in support of existing resource sharing. In these cases, members end up having to ship with the expensive and slow United States Postal Service (USPS). A series of three Colorado-based surveys conducted over ten years all found substantial savings to participating libraries that used that state's courier system. In 2012, for example, the Colorado delivery survey found that moving nearly six million items a year costs $900,000, much less than the $4,700,000 it would have cost to ship by USPS or the $8,000,000 it would have cost to ship by UPS or FedEx. The studies can be found at www.lrs.org/2012/03/13/high-traffic-low-cost-the-colorado-courier-continues-to-save-libraries-millions-annually-in-shipping-charges.

For many years, physical delivery had skyrocketed. For example, Massachusetts saw a 38-fold increase in deliveries over 21 years. This trend has changed in recent years, with most libraries couriers reporting flat usage or slight declines. The exception to this trend is when a resource-sharing networking adds a new direct patron-placed requesting system. Allowing patrons to request items always causes a large borrowing surge. Other trends in delivery include expanding multistate delivery and automated materials handling. To learn more about delivery, join ALA ASCLA's Physical Delivery Interest Group, or check out *Moving Materials: Physical Delivery in Libraries* by Valerie Horton and Bruce Smith. Chapter 6 goes into more detail about physical delivery services.

Resource Sharing

Depending on how the resource-sharing service is established, it can be one of the largest staffing units in a consortium. Some cooperatives manage interlibrary loan systems, coordinate with other partner organizations, and run a delivery service with only a few staff members. In other consortia, the staff may actually find and retrieve requested items in addition to the tasks mentioned above. In such cases staffing may be substantially larger. Overall, many changes are occurring in resource sharing. Chapter 5 goes into this topic in depth.

Consortia Support Agencies

There are a few organizations that provide support for consortia. ASCLA typically presents a number of programs geared towards consortia management at most ALA conferences. ASCLA's Consortia Management Discussion

Interest Group meets at the annual conference and is a good place to meet colleagues. The group focuses on funding, advocacy, and services for all types of library cooperatives. LYRASIS often hosts a consortia meeting at the ALA annual conference as well as hosting an additional annual meeting elsewhere in the country. Topics are selected by attendees.

Another significant and helpful resource for consortia managers is the International Coalition of Library Consortia (ICOLC). This informal self-organized group is unaffiliated with any organization, though LYRASIS generously provides help with logistics. It is international in scope and has both small and large consortia members that serve all types of libraries. At this writing, ICOLC has approximately 200 member consortia, most from North America. The website lists ICOLC's function as "facilitating discussion on issues of common interest. Twice per year ICOLC conducts meetings dedicated to keeping participating consortia informed about new electronic information resources, pricing practices of electronic information providers and vendors, and other issues of importance to directors, governing boards, and libraries of consortia. From time to time ICOLC also issues statements regarding topics which affect libraries and library consortia." At ICOLC meetings a consortia manager can meet peers, learn about new trends and services, and discover what other organizations are doing.

Conclusion

The previous two chapters highlighted most major functions of library consortia as identified in several recent surveys. However the list is not meant to be exhaustive. A number of consortia operate in niche roles providing one very specific function. Amherst College's high-density storage device service is an example, and we have included a case study that examines it.

Other consortia that engage in many common services may also provide one unusual service. SUNY's e-textbook system is an example of a rather unique service, and we have included a case study of it. The Massachusetts Library Networks' temporary employment service also provides a unique service. In chapters 3 and 4 and in the case studies, we have provided a snapshot of the range of vibrant services offered to libraries by their consortia.

Notes

1. Denis M. Davis, "Library Networks, Cooperatives and Consortia: A National Survey," 2007, www.ala.org/offices/sites/ala.org.offices/files/content/ors/lncc/interim_report_1_may2006.pdf.
2. Denise Pan and Yem Fong, "Return on Investment for Collaborative Collection Development: A Cost-Benefit Evaluation of Consortia Purchasing," *Collaborative Librarianship* 2, no. 4 (2010): 183–192.
3. Karen Calhoun, et al., *Online Catalogs: What Users and Librarians Want: An OCLC Report* (2009).
4. Valerie Horton and Bruce Smith, *Moving Materials: Physical Delivery in Libraries* (Chicago: American Library Association, 2010).

CHAPTER 5

Discovery, E-content Delivery, and Resource Sharing

Tracey Leger-Hornby and Greg Pronevitz

Many of the consortial services described in chapter 4 are components of discovery to delivery, and, at the same time, components of resource sharing. These consortial services include consortial hosting of shared integrated library systems (ILS), consortial management of shared licensing and collections, physical delivery services, interlibrary loan, and document delivery. Consortia play a leading role as resource-sharing facilitators, in centralizing negotiations and licensing, and in creating economies of scale to leverage limited member resources.

In the next two chapters, we examine the present state and the future of discovery to delivery. This chapter focuses on the general topic of discovery and its integral relationship to the delivery of electronic content. Discovery and delivery of e-content are in a constant state of development. This chapter begins with a discussion of the changing nature of library content, including the opportunities and challenges posed by e-books and open-access content. This introduction is followed by a look at discovery tools past, present, and future. We include a review of two critical aspects of discovery to delivery—authentication of library users and vendor relationships. In chapter 6 we will look at physical delivery of library materials in detail. While e-content is rapidly becoming mainstream in libraries, the need to ship traditional library materials between libraries to support resource sharing is likely to remain an essential service provided by many consortia for years to come. Many opportunities exist to improve the efficiency and quality of physical delivery services and related library workflows.

This pairing of discovery and delivery is a necessity if libraries are to compete for attention and resources in an era rich with other information providers. In virtually all cases the curated content provided by libraries has more value and a higher cost than the content that is available on the web with a quick search and click at no charge. Libraries have much work to do to promote and demonstrate the value of their content because library discovery to delivery usually requires more effort than a simple search and click. We must meet the challenge of providing services to meet the needs of users who are often unwilling and sometimes unable to take the steps required to access library content. We must also inform users who often are unaware of the existence and value of library content.

Even the best-endowed and strongest-resourced libraries cannot go it alone. Libraries are champions of resource sharing and of going the extra mile for our patrons. Libraries are often able to provide discovery and delivery of multilibrary content. Consortia support resource sharing with services and connections. However, our resource-sharing future has grown more challenging because copyright law does not govern our right to lend electronic content purchased under a license. Consortia are involved in negotiations for online access with more limited rights and even prohibitions on lending. Often, the right to lend materials to our consortial partners and other libraries is more restrictive than under copyright law.

Content, Collections, and Format

Library collections include a wide range of content, including monographs, journals, stories, articles, music, indexes, images, games, ephemera, and more. In recent times formats have evolved quickly. Monographs have gone from a paper book to audio recording on cassette, CD, or in downloadable format such as MP3, and now to digitized formats. A variation of the downloadable format is the digital file for short-term loan or purchase-on-demand.

The content of the monograph is much the same as it has been for centuries, yet the format and means of delivery continue to change. The content of the monograph may change, too, in light of new presentation opportunities in electronic formats. When a monograph becomes a digital file, there is another significant change. Copyright law may be superseded when the digital file is purchased under a license.

Libraries continue to purchase music collections in twentieth century formats, (e.g., compact discs), but they also buy in streaming format under a license or purchase individual songs for patron download on demand. More new formats and delivery mechanisms are inevitable.

The evolution from copyright to license has introduced new pricing pressures to the public library market. Public libraries were accustomed to a significant discount on the retail price for books. The introduction of e-book licensing brought with it lower prices for individual customers and higher pricing and/or restrictions on use and sharing for library purchases. Even the term "purchase" has become debatable as content providers include restrictions on the use of the digital file in library licenses.

Copyright and licensing implications are likely to play a major role in the future of library services and library consortial activities. Library consortia traditionally include a component of resource sharing or group purchasing, which is one of their most popular services. Only five consortia of the 59 that listed specific services in our 2012 survey did not engage in resource sharing. Discovery and delivery are essential components of resource sharing. Shared collections and generous sharing among consortium members are efficient uses of resources and a long tradition among libraries.

Building Twenty-First Century Collections

The evolution from print books and other physical media to electronic format has been rapid in academic libraries. In public libraries the transition to electronic books and downloadable media has been slower. Parallel services for e-content among consortia have been led by academic library consortia. Now public library consortia are entering the landscape, and the change is accelerating.

One of the best-known pioneering efforts to expand consortial access to academic library content is OhioLINK. An early concept in this project was to follow the example of the Harvard University depository to avoid construction and land use on main campuses for storage of library materials. This led to the construction of five regional high-density storage facilities.

This activity was accompanied by the development of user-friendly patron-placed hold capability for traditional library materials in 89 academic institutions. OhioLINK's innovative and wide-ranging consortial success also included statewide licensing and/or statewide advantageous pricing opportunities for a large assortment of electronic journals and databases. Some content was housed on OhioLINK servers.[1]

Group licensing for index and database content is now common, and many consortia offer this service. In some cases it is the main reason for the consortium's existence. Shared collections and collaborative collection development is another widespread service provided by consortia, including 67 percent of consortia that responded to our survey.

Aggregation and Licensing of E-book Content

Many academic libraries have incorporated e-book content within discovery platforms that integrate metadata from multiple formats, and in the best case scenario, require a single log-in to facilitate discovery. Academic libraries tend to purchase from ProQuest, EBSCO, Ingram, and directly from publishers of academic content such as Springer and Elsevier.

Public libraries and their patrons are still struggling with multiple logins, unfriendly user interfaces, and an untapped audience that doesn't know that the e-book service exists or is dissatisfied with the process and content selection. OverDrive, the market leader in public libraries, has made inroads with many library consortia with first sales and later with licensing of e-books to groups. Other aggregators who primarily serve public libraries include Baker & Taylor and 3M.

Discovery of e-books often takes place through the ILS in both academic and public libraries. Academic library users also routinely find e-books through commercially available discovery platforms. Delivery differs by library type and vendor. Academic libraries tend to purchase e-books that are licensed for one or more simultaneous users, and a proxy server is often the authentication mechanism. For public libraries, a checkout procedure on the vendor platform is normally required when digital rights management (DRM) systems are used to ensure license compliance.

Various commercial platforms provide different levels of user friendliness for the checkout. Improving this procedure has been a goal in the public library community for several years. The first generation platforms and integration of DRM with early e-reader devices such as the Nook and Kindle were challenging.

Group licensing for e-books is in its early stages and still evolving. Ownership and the right to transfer to new platforms of e-books is a major issue, especially in public libraries. Some aggregators require the use of their own platform to assure permanent access. Therefore, if a library decides not to use a particular vendor platform, the past investment in owned content on that platform may be lost. The major aggregators that claim to offer ownership or permanent access say they will assist the library or consortia in communicating with publishers to allow the transfer of titles to a new platform. Aggregators explain that the publishers have the final say.

Jo Budler of the Kansas State Library made headlines in the library press when she decided to transfer owned content from one aggregator to another. She said the process was labor intensive.

Jamie LaRue, formerly of Douglas County Libraries (CO), has inspired replication of the model developed by his team for self-hosted e-books, which provides the clearest ownership. LaRue developed a simple two-page statement of common understanding that replicates the ownership and rights of a traditional book, providing for library pricing along with the ability to purchase additional copies should use levels demand it. Perpetual access or ownership and the right to transfer content among technology platforms for e-books is as important as delivery in some cases.

The third major issue is pricing. Libraries, aggregators, and publishers must settle on fair prices for library access. The Douglas County model, for example, not only simplifies the user experience, it allows libraries to circumvent the aggregator, reducing some costs while putting technology management and development into the hands of libraries. On a consortial scale, with centralized management, support, training, and shared costs, such a model is worth exploring.

The number of consortia that are developing e-book platforms based on the Douglas County Model continues to grow, including Amigos Library Services, CALIFA, Marmot, and NC LIVE. A working group in Colorado is seeking to improve upon the model. A commercial development effort is underway with OdiloTID, a company that was a technology partner with Douglas County Libraries, with branches in Spain, Mexico, and the United States. The Queens Library plans to seek an alternative platform based on a commercial platform. These efforts demonstrate that the models provided by aggregators are not meeting consortial needs.

Another e-book model in widespread use is the annual lease of a collection of e-books on a commercial platform. This vendor-based model allows instant delivery of e-content that publishers are willing to license to libraries. Ownership is not an issue with a leasing model. In many ways, it is similar to an annual license to a database-type product that includes full-text articles. Leased e-book prices will vary depending on the user base size and library type and on content quality and age. OverDrive, an e-book lease-system vendor popular with public libraries, provides access to numerous consortia for collections of e-books. In the academic library sphere, ProQuest's EBL and ebrary are popular services. A popular crossover vendor in both environments is Safari.

The patron-driven acquisition model (PDA) is a third model for e-books. These are also referred to as demand-driven acquisitions or DDA. PDA systems may be combined with a short-term loan program. In the combined scenario, a collection of catalog records and/or metadata is made discoverable through the library's ILS and/or discovery system. The collection includes many more titles than the library is likely to want to purchase. Patrons discover a title and request delivery of the item. Various levels of use trigger a short-term loan, including pages viewed or printed, time spent reading the item, or multiple uses. Vendors set a threshold for short-term loans that creates a purchase in collaboration with the library. Here again the question of transferability of an "owned" title comes into play. Libraries don't have a lot of experience with such transfers. Testing of consortial PDA models is in progress with several academic consortia, including Orbis-Cascade Alliance, The Virtual Library of Virginia (VIVA), and MOBIUS (a multitype library consortium in Missouri).

ILL is a challenge when the first-sale doctrine is eliminated and restrictive licensing provisions prohibit this popular library activity. Many publishers in the academic arena allow limited ILL. This is not true for the publishers that sell chiefly to public libraries. This is an area that needs to be addressed by library consortia if they are to continue to facilitate resource sharing.

We still have a long way to go in providing a user-friendly, affordable option for e-books in libraries. After the e-book platform issue is resolved satisfactorily, libraries will undoubtedly be facing new formats, new business models, and other exciting new opportunities to deliver state-of-the-art content to users.

Open-Access Content

The cost of commercial scientific publishing is borne to a large extent by libraries. The Scholarly Publishing and Academic Resources Coalition (SPARC®) was formed in the late 1990s by an alliance of academic libraries to create a more open system of scholarly communication. There is a growing trend toward the creation of scholarly open-access materials. While commercial content is likely to remain protected by copyright and license terms for many years, the option for open content is being investigated and tested. The long-term business model for open-access content is still unknown.

The University of California's Academic Senate established an open-access policy in 2013 to fulfill its commitment to disseminating its research and scholarship widely. This step is not unique. However, it is significant in that it covers some 8,000 scholars on ten campuses. It is included, along with 120 additional US entries, in ROARMAP.org (a worldwide Registry of Open Access Repositories Mandatory Archiving Policies). Models for open-access licensing are in development at www.CreativeCommons.org and www.LibraryLicense.org.

Open Archives Initiative's (OAI) harvesting and searching are being employed to provide access to collections of open content through institutional repositories. For example the Bielefeld Academic Search Engine (BASE) recently hit a milestone by indexing more than 50 million OAI-records across 2,700 repositories.

Discovery Tools

The librarian's historical role is to acquire, provide access to, and preserve knowledge since ancient times when knowledge was stored on papyrus scrolls. Development of a system to share cataloging data and create catalog cards efficiently led to the formation of the largest library consortium—OCLC, in 1967. The early online public access catalogs (OPAC) library systems were modeled on the traditional card catalog. Librarians needed to train users to use the tools based on complex rules and unfriendly taxonomies. However patrons could always approach a librarian at the reference desk to ask for help.

A shared OPAC became a consortial staple with early projects such as the North of Boston Library Exchange (NOBLE), which was founded as a multilibrary system in 1980 in Massachusetts, and CLEVNET, which was a multilibrary system founded in 1982 in northeast Ohio. OhioLINK introduced a groundbreaking statewide initiative with a large-scale virtual catalog that facilitated patron-initiated borrowing across catalogs in 1992.

Shared ILSs are common now as are virtual catalog systems, connecting multiple systems for patron-initiated requests. Cutting-edge projects include the Orbis-Cascade Alliance's single shared ILS and vision of a shared electronic collection for its 37 academic library members, and multitype library connections in Michigan that employ a virtual catalog connector for more than 400 multitype libraries with MeLCat, a project of the Library of Michigan.

As discovery was simplified with these systems, delivery became more complex. The popularity of patron-initiated holds caused a huge increase in the volume of requests for delivery in the early 2000s. Consortia that provided physical delivery were overwhelmed. The increase in volume spawned service issues and pricing crises for consortia and libraries. Consortial leaders responded by calling two national conferences on physical delivery called Moving Mountains, by forming an American Library Association Physical Delivery Interest Group, and by publishing numerous articles and a book on the subject. Physical delivery is covered in more detail in chapter 6.

For library users searching for journal or magazine articles, the discovery process followed a similar path from print to computer. Libraries subscribed to a relatively small number of indexing and abstracting services and individual journal titles. Online tools simplified the process by providing keyword searches, indexing, and abstracts in one spot. Print copies of the individual articles were not always at hand. This was a barrier to delivery. Interlibrary loan and document delivery services helped.

As indexing and abstracting services moved online, a trend developed to aggregate more content into a single interface. Early tools—Silver Platter, InfoTrac, and Dialog—became the front end for searching periodical literature. The early OPACs aggregated back office operations and made it possible to see if an issue of a journal had arrived, whether a book was checked out or available, if a book was on order, and if a book was on the shelf. Still the separation between book and periodical remained.

Technology to search multiple systems emerged, leveraging the growing volume of digital content and expanded use of the Internet. Early book searching using National Information Standards Organization's (NISO) Z39.50 protocol, and federated article searching such as Ex Libris' MetaLib service let users view results from many sources simultaneously.

The next tool to link the citation and object was the link-resolver. This tool connects the library user to the content by storing technical information such as the URL on the library side of the transaction; the IP address to authenticate the user is stored on the vendor side. Ex Libris was an early adopter, using the product SFX. Periodical literature was first to be widely digitized. Tools moved from index-only to full-text in a few short years and resources became easily accessible by the end user.

Academic publishers moved to pricing models that required purchase of both print and online versions of the titles they produced. Libraries found little budget relief from the shift to online resources. Producers also began experimenting with package deals to test markets. For many libraries the allure of having more titles while removing print copies from overcrowded shelves was too hard to resist. It is now unusual to purchase single indexes or single digital journal subscriptions. Large-scale efforts to reduce print, such as Project MUSE and JSTOR, were systematic and explicit in their attempt to reduce the need to access print by providing online content. Library consortia jumped on the bandwagon for content packages with group purchasing opportunities. Even the biggest deals are now available and negotiated by consortia (see Case Study 5, Embracing Wide Deals).

When the emerging commercial giants Google and Amazon introduced the simple search box, it became easier to use the Internet to find information. Alternatives and suggestions for incorrect spelling helped guide web searchers. Users liked the simplicity.

Retailers such as Sears offered a new online experience with faceted searching that has become the model for information seeking. Want to buy a stove? Use facets to limit the search results to electric or gas models. The same techniques help narrow a library search; just pick a language, a year of publication, and a format. In early OPAC systems, advanced searching to narrow the results was possible but not simple. Library users needed to take several extra steps and know exactly what they wanted to be able to perform a complex search. Keyword versus controlled vocabulary was also an issue. Users do not want to look up terms or use formal syntax to find what they need. Many OPAC systems introduced keywords to assist users in finding materials with more natural language. Semantic search algorithms behind the scenes help, but they are not always enough to tease out obscure topics or highly specialized works. Over time, most libraries made keyword searching a default strategy and began the process of moving formal subject headings into near obscurity for most library users.

Issues for librarians include simultaneously trying to get patrons to use the discovery tools if they need a general starting point for research and directing them to specific tools for a narrowly focused inquiry. When a high school student needs a reference for a research paper, a simple search using basic tools can be successful. A graduate student writing a doctoral dissertation requires specialized tools and unique resources. A single search box as an entry to millions of individual objects will produce results and may guide the user to tools that are more sophisticated. If the intent is to start a narrow and specialized search, the wide-scope of a common discovery tool may not be effective, and in fact, may be very frustrating.

Discovery is not the silver bullet; it is a moving target. As soon as one version of software is in place, the next is in the pipeline. The pace for changes in interface and structure for library tools is no different from the pace of other software packages. Libraries face challenges keeping documentation and training materials up-to-date as the vendors shift to agile software development versus traditional periodic updates with major incremental improvements.

Lorcan Dempsey gives an excellent overview of the development of catalogs and discovery tools in his article "Thirteen Ways of Looking at Libraries, Discovery, and the Catalog: Scale, Workflow, Attention" in the December 2012 issue of *EDUCAUSE Review*. Dempsey points out the need for and potential development of new ways of sharing resources. These include following examples in other markets, such as community tagging, adding reviews, recommendation services, and exposing library data for expanded access via search engines. He also points to improved intersystem collaboration between vendors and libraries, including Google linking to holdings information in OCLC "find a library" links in book results lists.

Another useful overview of the marketplace is Marshall Breeding's annual *Library Journal* article on library systems. Breeding analyzes the trends, tools, and market swings. His opinions are highly valued, and he provides clear descriptions of the technical aspects of the tools. The current market leaders in library discovery markets, according to Breeding, are Summon, Primo, EBSCO Discovery Service, and OCLC WorldShare.

The Orbis-Cascade Alliance announced a major step forward in consortial discovery for its members in October 2012. Its 37 members are migrating to a shared use of Primo with many shared sources of metadata as a discovery tool and the cloud-based Alma as an ILS.

High-quality relevancy of search results is a key goal in discovery. The discovery software market is evolving, as is the array of features and user interfaces. Google is the primary competition with its single search box. In academic libraries some believe that Google Scholar is a viable alternative to commercial products with appropriate linking set up behind-the-scenes.

The process behind discovery systems involves gathering top-level information (citation, abstract, and descriptors) on content, whether that is a book, a peer-reviewed scholarly article, or a photograph in an archive. The collection of the information is structured and indexed by the discovery vendor, and it is normalized or formatted to a common syntax; finally duplicates are removed. The magic part of the process is how the software then takes massive amounts of data and finds the most relevant items to match the search terms entered by the user.

Each vendor has different mechanisms to find the matching items and usually offers some customization that allows the library choice in whether or not to put certain items up front. For example, some libraries want the print or electronic book collection results first before articles. Libraries provide vendors with lists of licensed subscription materials (journals, databases, electronic book collections) and items they want users to find. This includes web pages with library hours, guides to finding materials by topic or subject areas, and local special collections.

Authentication

The way in which libraries connect users with a wide range of items found in discovery systems is constrained by licensing agreements that vary by product. Most library systems have built-in procedures to verify users. Users must enter information to confirm their identities and present credentials to gain access to licensed materials. Libraries can decide where to put the authentication barrier or wall within the discovery experience.

Worcester Polytechnic Institute (WPI) and other libraries allow anyone on the web to access the discovery search service. Anyone can look at the list of results from a search, but only authenticated WPI users can see licensed content. The authentication process ensures adherence to the university's license agreements for distribution of materials to authorized users only. Some libraries put the wall before the search service and do not allow anyone outside to see content or to complete a search.

Challenges to user-friendly authentication grow in complexity when members of a library consortia use a single discovery system to differentiate local users from consortial users. Some statewide projects, including the iConn site in Connecticut (http://iconn.org) and the Massachusetts libraries site (http://mass.gov/libraries), employ geolocation to bring down the wall for all in-state users by allowing access to any computer with an in-state IP address. However, this geolocation does not allow for local access to locally licensed content. The Boston Public Library provides a statewide e-card that is available online on demand. This inventive model provides timely access to locally licensed content to all residents of Massachusetts.

Two large Canadian municipal public library systems recently reported on their study of public library patrons and their discovery software experience. The title of their report indicates the direction they see library systems moving. "Social Discovery Systems in Public Libraries: If We Build Them, Will They Come?" by Louise F. Spiteri and Laurel Tarulli was published in *Library Trends* 61/1. The study investigated patron interactions not just with the libraries' resources but with each other and the library staff. They found users were hesitant to use some of the tools and suggested they may be using commercial products such as Goodreads Inc. and software instead.

When faced with the choice to join the social interaction movement or remain within traditional library practices, these two systems jumped into new territory and investigated what they call social discovery systems. They state, "Most extant usability studies provide important insight into how people interact with online catalogues and how these experiences can be improved; what becomes evident from these studies is that catalogues should reflect the information needs and terminology of users, rather than library staff." The study looked at transaction logs and other relevant usage-tracking data. The findings indicated that users did not make good use of the social tools provided by the library. The authors speculate that a probable cause might be the long-held stereotype that interactions with a library are limited to simply requesting items and engaging in typical circulation activities

Academic library use of discovery systems and other interactions with library resources has also been investigated. In the recently released *Ithaka S+R US Faculty Survey* (2012; www.sr.ithaka.org/research-publications/us-faculty-survey-2012), the authors questioned faculty on the use of library resources and tools they use to do their scholarly research. They found that for known-item searches, 40 percent of responding faculty started with the library web page. About 30 percent moved directly to a scholarly database rather than the library's general search tools. Another 20 percent used a general-purpose search engine, and only a small portion of faculty sought out a librarian to assist with the search. They report further that there are variations on the search strategies according to discipline.

Academic libraries face the reality of dwindling use of print collections. Public libraries are experiencing a leveling off of or small decline in circulation of print and media after a decade of significant growth. There is an expectation that use is likely to decline further as physical media is supplanted by downloadable and streaming options. Library building use, however, is growing steadily in both academic and public libraries.

In academic libraries students working in groups, seeking quiet study space, or needing technology come into libraries in droves. This trend to install information commons with rich technology is forcing examination of the need to store thousands of print books in library buildings that are now starving for more collaboration and teaching spaces. Rick Lugg, president of Sustainable Collections Services and a nationally recognized authority on collections management, notes, "It's surprising how often the questions of discovery and delivery surface in discussions about deselection. Whether the goal is sharing, weeding, or storage, librarians want to be sure that this content can be found and obtained in the unlikely event that it is needed."

A new and critical function of the discovery systems of tomorrow may be their role as facilitator or delivery agent between individual users with larger repositories of materials that are no longer housed in separate libraries. Jay Schafer, director of the University of Massachusetts's Amherst Library, states, "It is clear that as the library community moves forward with a variety of depository/off site shelving solutions, it will be essential that we are able to create a national discovery tool to aid in knowing what is being housed where." The University of Massachusetts's Amherst DuBois Library is part of the Five College libraries group, which has been working on collaborative collection building and sharing for many years (see also Case Study 12, Shared Physical Depository: The Five College Library Depository). Their book storage strategy is under review at the moment as they grapple with ways to ensure both discovery and delivery of books in a new era of limited holdings.

The days of measuring a library's success and stature by the number of books in the building are past and new standards of assessing library value are in development. The Association of College & Research Libraries sponsored research and publication of a comprehensive review of the shifting trends in assessing the value of academic libraries by Megan Oakleaf.[2]

Public library use is strong. Pew Internet and Life reported that 53 percent of Americans visited libraries or bookmobiles at least once in the past year. Browsing and borrowing books and media were the most popular activities in a January 2013 survey, "Library Services in the Digital Age." In Massachusetts, total annual public library visits are up 50 percent since 2000, while the level of borrowing and interlibrary loans has been stable for three years after a decade of very strong growth.

Relationships

A major issue in the current state of the discovery tool marketplace is relationships with publishers and information providers. In order to make items available to library users, the discovery tool software providers negotiate with publishers to obtain metadata. The general concept is that by having publishers make the indexing and citations accessible, more potential users will discover and perhaps purchase the materials than if the content and metadata is available to only licensed libraries. However, that theory does not hold true for all types of materials or all publishers. Some vendors do not make all collections available to other discovery software vendors. Some vendors are testing new business models; JSTOR for example, is now offering to provide services to individual researchers.

Finally, Asher, Duke, and Wilson have begun the evaluation of discovery tools in the academic library. They surveyed students using different discovery tools and assessed their success.[3] They used quantitative and qualitative methods to investigate strategies and outcomes of those using the tools. "Judging from these results, it seems that one of the most important and perhaps the single most important factor in determining which resources students will utilize is the default way in which a particular search system ranks and returns results," the authors reported. No matter their level of preparation or expertise, the students participating in the study preferred tools that provide instant access to full-text results. Students seem to prefer to find items first and then evaluate them. Not surprisingly, most students did not move past the first page or two of results, and most performed searches that were not precise and so returned vast numbers of results.

Collaborative collection building and resource sharing are key strategies used in Maine and especially among the Colby, Bates, and Bowdoin (CBB) libraries to ensure that students and faculty have access to the materials they need in a timely manner. By drastically decreasing duplication of materials across the libraries, providing immediate discovery via a shared catalog and offering unmediated user borrowing and expedited delivery services, the libraries are better positioned to build collections to support dynamic curriculums and to embrace new digital formats.

The Maine Shared Collection Strategies project includes CBB libraries along with other partners, including Maine's largest public libraries, to develop a statewide strategy for print monograph and journal storage, retention, and preservation. Individual efforts, perhaps led by consortia and megaconsortia, throughout the country may someday serve as regional nodes, much like the distributed digital repositories that make up the Digital Public Library of America (DPLA), in a national effort.

If we broaden the scope of the rule beyond books to include information and data, we may still apply them to the tools and programs discussed here. Discovery and delivery are central components of library practice. The growth and rights issues of electronic resources present a challenge to library consortia that are dedicated to resource sharing.

Conclusion and Consortial Implications

The most sophisticated discovery systems are being employed in larger libraries and library systems and in a growing number of consortia.

Academic libraries have employed the most advanced technology. Some large public libraries are employing contemporary discovery tools, and some academic consortia are experimenting with the latest versions of shared discovery layers. The efficiency and quality of shared discovery platforms deserves attention and examination. As commercial discovery platforms become more mainstreamed and the large academic library market is saturated, we believe these platforms will become affordable to more libraries and consortia of all sizes, both academic and public. This service may prove very useful as it integrates searching for all, or almost all, library materials. A well-designed discovery tool should enhance the customer experience.

Shared discovery of physical and e-content combined with effective authentication systems and statistical reporting will allow consortia members to take best advantage of group purchasing, support, training, development, and perhaps most of all, efficiency.

The electronic materials sphere is expanding quickly and has strong patron interest. With some e-content, instant gratification is not difficult for the library to provide. Here again trends in academic and public libraries differ. Academic libraries tend to authenticate users with a proxy server. This trend can allow for a single log-on to instantly view content on multiple e-content platforms.

Proprietary platforms used by aggregators and the associated digital rights management (DRM) technology are significant barriers to delivery of e-books in the public library setting. In most libraries the content from different vendors is on a separate platform, and each system requires a separate log-in or check-out process to read or download an e-book. Technology solutions are in development with a 3M/Polaris joint effort for seamless e-book checkout, BiblioCommons integration with ILSs, and APIs to integrate various platforms and ILS.

Developing win-win relationships between consortia, aggregators, publishers, and authors to facilitate effective delivery of e-books in this setting is needed. Some major publishers were reluctant to sell popular e-books to public libraries as the technology was introduced. The resistance seems to be declining, and new models are being developed and tested. New aggregators have come on the scene with new models for delivery. Library consortia such as CALIFA and NC LIVE are setting up consortial e-book servers and working directly with publishers to purchase content. Libraries and consortia may have an opportunity to develop relationships directly with authors and other content creators to become publishers of e-content without any intermediaries.

Librarians need to reflect on the purpose, use, and effectiveness of discovery tools that promise to provide an enhanced user experience. They must also decide if the investment in building and purchasing discovery tools is worth the time and money. Communications and/or training about both the benefits and the limitations of discovery tools is also essential. It is likely that discovery tools will evolve and improve over time. Consortia and members must also consider when and if joint investment in such tools will be more efficient and effective for member libraries and patrons.

Notes

1. Randy Dykhuis, "OhioLINK: Vision, Money, and Technology," *Computers in Libraries* 15, no. 2 (1995).
2. Megan Oakleaf, *Value of Academic Libraries: A Comprehensive Research Review and Report* (Chicago: Association of College & Research Libraries, 2010).
3. Andrew D. Asher, Lynda M. Duke, and Suzanne Wilson, "Paths of Discovery: Comparing the Search Effectiveness of EBSCO Discovery Service, Summon, Google Scholar, and Conventional Library Resources," *College & Research Libraries* 74, no. 5: (September 2013): 464–488.

CHAPTER 6

Physical Delivery: Future and Present

Lori Bowen Ayre and Greg Pronevitz

We briefly described physical delivery in chapter 4 and in chapter 5, where we focused on discovery and delivery of e-content. This chapter focuses on the state-of-the-art in physical delivery and logistics. There is still a strong need to ship items from library to library or to the patron, as part of library resource sharing, and it is likely to remain essential for many years. More than half of respondents to our consortial survey provide physical delivery services to member libraries This service is very popular among patrons. Traditional library collections will be important to libraries and patrons for a long time.

Like discovery, delivery is a moving target. Discovery drives the demand for delivery. The user discovers something; the user wants it. It used to be that finding the item was enough. But today, user expectations have collapsed the discovery and the delivery steps into one fulfillment step.

The Future of Delivery

One day, libraries will be able to generate a copy of a book or video for a user on the spot. Libraries will move more and more items out of the library and into high-density storage systems, where it is much cheaper to store them and to quickly retrieve them for patrons. For patrons that are not onsite, it might require a few extra minutes to retrieve the book, digitize it, and send the digital surrogate, but it will still be nearly instantaneous.

To comply with copyright and licensing issues, the digital surrogate will eventually serve as a circulation of that physical item and contain a Digital Rights Management (DRM) code to ensure that it circulates back to the library after a defined circulation period.

We are still in the very early stages of this scenario. Print-on-demand technologies such as the Espresso Machine are available but are not affordable for library-scale use, and digitization-on-demand isn't viable for mainstream use yet. However, in the commercial sphere, Internet booksellers are printing on demand and shipping the same day, and most book buyers are unaware that their book was printed just for them. Physical delivery of library material will continue to be a core library service until the technology catches up. And even then, we may still be waiting for the copyright and licensing battles to be resolved.

For libraries to take full advantage of digitization-on-demand, a number of changes must take place. Copyright law must be interpreted in such a way as to allow the above-mentioned transaction. Or, in an ideal world, publishers will grant permission for such work in particular situations. Perhaps the library could turn over the digital file to the publisher in exchange for ongoing use; the publisher could then resell that digital copy in digital or as print-on-demand form. Libraries might see significant cost savings, and the item might see dramatically increased use, particularly if the use turns into a citation in an important publication.

Discovery to delivery is predominantly electronic in many academic libraries, though academic books are still routinely shipped around the country. The proportion of electronic transactions is growing in public libraries as well. The volume of shipping for loans of traditional library materials among consortia members has not grown for three years. Delivery managers anticipate a gradual decline over the next few years and a steeper decline further out as media-based library materials such as movies on DVD, music on CD, and books on CD are delivered via streaming or a download. Media typically make up 30–40 percent of consortial shipping among public libraries. Books have become a smaller and smaller part of library circulation as spending on books has shrunk. As of 2010, 31 percent of public library circulation was comprised of videos and DVDs.[1]

State-of-the-Art Physical Delivery

While waiting for an idyllic future, consortia and libraries still need to operate courier services that move many millions of items a year. That's because every library relies on other libraries to fill patron requests, usually through reciprocal borrowing relationships and interlibrary loan. While there are many reasons that the circulation and interlibrary loan of physical materials are expected to decline, the huge stocks of books, DVDs, and CDs on library shelves will still have high value to patrons for some time. Patrons are still discovering the title they want and requesting it. This triggers a chain of events to get the item to patrons at the pick-up location they specified.

Libraries pay direct and indirect costs to provide delivery. Libraries purchase, process, and shelve their materials. They participate in consortial catalogs to make technology cost effective and to expand access for patrons. They provide the housing and labor costs to pull, process, and ship books, and when a book is returned, they pay to process and reshelve the item as well.

Still, the costs associated with consortial borrowing are significantly cheaper than traditional mediated interlibrary loan transactions (ILL). The cost of an ILL transaction has been documented and tends to hover around $25–$30 per transaction; the library labor costs for a typical intraconsortial transaction, however, can be as low as $3. Delivery costs alone are often significantly cheaper. Couriers, whether outsourced or not, generally cost less than a first-class postage stamp per item delivered round-trip in high-volume environments and only a dollar or two in lower-volume systems.

Outsourcing vs. In-House Delivery

Many consortia outsource delivery and sorting services to commercial firms. There are pros and cons to outsourcing. Internal courier services can be more flexible in terms of scheduling and accommodating library closures and staffing fluctuations. Libraries report fewer losses and less damage when using employee couriers.

There are drawbacks to in-house delivery. Investment in vehicles, sorting equipment, and warehouse space is costly and long-term. Hiring management and staff to perform the work also has long-term implications, particularly in unionized and public-employer environments. Purchasing the proper vehicle, setting up efficient systems, and deploying staff effectively requires much experience. Quality commercial couriers have experience and are able to allocate personnel and equipment more efficiently and usually get the job done at a lower cost.

Another benefit of using a regional courier is competition. An effective procurement process and contract ensure reliable, cost-effective performance. Also, regional couriers have multiple customers and have the ability to add drivers and vehicles as needed. Finally, some consortia couriers comingle library material with other deliveries, which may further reduce overall costs if volume allows.

Whether managing an outsourced regional courier or an in-house fleet of drivers, it is important to be proactive. Outsourcing does not mean giving up responsibility for the service. For example, it is important to ensure that deliveries happen on schedule so libraries can align staffing appropriately. Interlibrary deliveries should be a top priority for library staff.

Bulk shipment of library material from library to library is more cost-effective and less labor-intensive than using package delivery providers like United Parcel Service (UPS) (or discounted UPS CampusShip) and FedEx—or even the US Postal Service (USPS), which offers lower cost Media Mail. The package pricing models don't work very well for libraries with large volume because their charges are complex and high, though some academic libraries prefer fast turnaround for critical materials for scholars. When costs for packing, unpacking, and the packaging materials are considered, package carrier costs are even higher. There is a tradeoff, however; the lower cost of couriers also brings a lower level of tracking ability and accountability.

Current Physical Delivery Challenges and Best Practices

The shared ILS and commercial discovery systems are the primary discovery systems, and they determine what patrons will discover and which patron will get which copy. In a resource-sharing environment in which multiple ILSs are interconnected with a consortial borrowing product, such as Autographics Share-It, RelaisD2D, Innovative's INN-Reach, or OCLC Navigator, it is the resource-sharing product that handles much discovery and targets requests based on a profile set up by the consortium. Coordination of the physical delivery system and the discovery tools can help make delivery more efficient. When the two systems get out-of-sync, imbalances and other problems may arise in the physical delivery system.

Two open-source ILSs offer features to enhance delivery efficiency. Koha developers recently added a transport cost matrix that allows each library to assign a cost for delivering to other locations in the system. Items selected to fill a request will look for the least costly method for that pick-up location. Evergreen employs a wait-and-see option called opportunistic capture that allows a request to remain unfulfilled for a window of time to see if the pickup location will check in the item. This option can relieve staff from the need to pull the item off the shelf and eliminate the need to transport it.

Sorting has always posed a challenge for libraries. In many consortia, sorting often has been left to library staff when volume is low and there is room for sorting and storage of a tote or bag for each location. A typical workflow in libraries is to check in returns, put routing slips on the ones that go elsewhere, and organize everything on book carts. Items that need to go "in transit" can be sorted into distribution totes, while the other material can get onto the local library shelves. However, when that library system becomes part of a larger or high-volume system composed of multiple locations, setting out one tote per location is no longer a viable approach. Instead, all materials are placed in mixed totes that are sorted at a central location. Many high-volume library delivery services have outgrown the in-library sorting method but continue to operate this way, as they have since the advent of shared ILSs in the 1980s.

One of the biggest breakthroughs in library sorting came with the introduction of the Seattle Public Library's automated materials handling (AMH) system in 2004. The Tech-Logic system installed that year included self-service check-in options for patrons, an elaborate conveyance system for getting the items to the sorting room, and a sorter that sorted items to a book cart or into a bin for delivery to branches. The system was based on radio frequency identification (RFID) that allowed the AMH system to quickly detect the RFID tag and poll the ILS for the associated "barcode" number on the item to determine the item's destination.

The breakthrough was not so much about the library's use of radio frequency identification (RFID) but more the idea of sorting based on barcode number instead of a routing label. Instead of having a human sorter reading the paper routing slip, the AMH system communicated with the ILS via the Standard Interchange Protocol (SIP). Labor costs for sorting were dramatically reduced. SIP was developed by 3M to support communication between external programs and the ILS to support self-check machines. Seattle's AMH used SIP to query the ILS about the status of the item being returned and to find out what should happen to it next. SIP is now on version 2.0, and the standard is managed by NISO. Virtually all AMH systems and self-check devices in use today rely on SIP2 to perform check-in and sorting.

Tote manifesting (creating an electronic manifest for a group of items collected together and sent in a tote) and batch check-in of interlibrary delivery items is supported by some ILSs, although the feature is a function of the AMH system, not the ILS. The King County Library System (KCLS) was the first library to use such a system. The sorter designed by Lyngsoe Library Systems sorts to more than 150 destinations and builds a manifest for each tote as items are sorted into it. Each of the 48 KCLS branches can then efficiently check totes in instead of checking in each item upon receipt.

AMH system use has become widespread. The largest installations are in large county and urban library systems. Consortial use is limited to a system shared by the New York Public Library and the Brooklyn Public Library as part of collaboration to share technical services and delivery. Consortia have not adopted AMH systems for delivery services because a financial return has not yet been demonstrated at the consortial level. Large library systems are able to justify the investment for several reasons, including the high cost of union labor in public libraries and severe urban space constraints. However, inconsistent barcodes/RFID systems and the large number of destinations needed add to the cost for a consortial AMH.

In 2012, the Massachusetts Library System took the concept of using a SIP2 communication to determine how items were sorted and applied it to a manual-sort operation. They were able to keep sorting costs low by cutting out the capital-intensive AMH. This reduction was done by equipping each human sorter with a wrist-worn scanner to read the item's barcode and query the ILS. The ILS reported destination data back to the sorting operation by means of a light-assisted sorting system. Above each sort location is a light that illuminates to indicate where a sorter should place an item.

This system, developed by Optima, a local courier, is based on a put-to-light system that is common in warehouse management. Optima was the first to adapt put-to-light to satisfy a library sorting operation. Optima has called it "sort-to-light." By eliminating the need to label each in-transit item, Optima's system considerably simplifies library workflow. "Label-less Library Logistics," an article in *Collaborative Librarianship*, describes the procurement process.[2]

Manually sorting library items involves a fair amount of handling, so reducing any unnecessary touches and steps is key to making the process efficient. When designing the sorting operation, best practices include clear labeling, especially to avoid confusion among destinations with similar names; angling totes; and tightly grouping totes into manageable sorting pods to eliminate as much walking as possible.

The packaging of in-transit items can have an effect on efficiency. Academic libraries are more inclined than public libraries to package items they put in transit because they are fragile, rare, valuable, and sometimes irreplaceable. Academic libraries also tend to ship a much smaller volume of materials. Public libraries usually transport popular material for which wear and tear is part of doing business. Obviously, protecting unique material is important. In general, however, use of jiffy bags or other packaging to protect material is less efficient. The key is to consider the replacement cost versus the burden on the library and delivery staff, the cost of the packaging itself, and the investment in labor to pack and unpack each item. Rather than using packaging, some consortia prefer training sorting staff to keep packaging to a minimum.

Libraries Are in the Logistics Business

Although many people would say that librarians shouldn't be in the logistics business, the truth is that they are. As long as we are filling requests for material from other libraries and allowing patrons to define their pick-up location, we have a logistics mandate. So, what does an excellent delivery service look like?

The best delivery system is the one that reduces delivery volume without sacrificing service to the patron. Many policies and procedures affect delivery volume, and finding the right balance is key to providing excellent service. For example, most libraries allow patrons to request items for pickup. As part of that service, they offer the patron a window of a few days to pick up the item before it is returned to the owning library. The number of items that libraries pull from the shelves, send to the pickup location, and place on the holds pickup shelves can be very high, and many of these items are never picked up. It takes a lot of work and costs a lot of money to get an item to a patron at another location, so reducing the number of expired holds that must be sent back to the owning library is something to strive for. Libraries may alleviate such issues by ensuring that patrons have enough time—but not too much—to pick up based on the notification method and clear instructions on how to freeze holds. As a last resort, the threat of a fine may lead to more pickups.

Another way to reduce delivery volume is to use floating collections, that is, allowing the item to stay where it is returned instead of sending it back through the delivery system to the owning library. Floating collections can dramatically reduce delivery volume, but they also require complex ongoing management. Floating collections have been used in self-contained library systems. We are not aware of consortial implementations.

Delivery volume can grow when holds are not managed well. It is important to closely monitor the behavior of the ILS to efficiently issue requests. It is best not to transport items from another library when they are available at the pickup location. Checking-in returns and interlibrary delivery items before printing the pull list is an easy way to reduce the size of the pull list because many of the requested items will be triggered at check-in. Working with library staff to coordinate when pull lists are generated and how often they are updated can have a positive effect on delivery volume and the resulting efficiencies.

Many libraries do not have room to spare. Therefore, more frequent deliveries with fewer totes per delivery are also recommended. Frequency of delivery must be balanced with other factors such as distance, available vehicles and drivers, and volume. Best practice is to deliver more frequent and smaller batches to the libraries whenever possible.

Designing delivery routes is more science than art. Several data elements, such as the storage capacity of the vehicle, the time needed to run the route, the length of route, time windows that need to be accommodated at each location, the number of vehicles, the number of drivers, and the hours each library is open and/or willing to accept delivery are all very important. Some couriers use route optimization software to plan delivery routes. This software is expensive and complex, and it is not always flexible enough for complicated library routes with day-to-day fluctuations in volume; however, it is important to monitor all factors and continually adjust routes as needed.

Radio Frequency Identification (RFID)

RFID technology holds the promise of improving materials handling and delivery services. New opportunities arose when the NISO released a new standard, RFID in US Libraries (RP-6-2012). Having a US data model to reference created an opportunity for libraries to achieve a degree of interoperability with RFID-tagged material.[3] It is possible for libraries to use different vendors to provide RFID-enabled products instead of being locked in with one vendor that provides all their RFID solutions. The guidelines also increase the likelihood that libraries switching from one ILS to another will be able to easily continue to use their RFID-enabled equipment. And finally, libraries using compliant RFID systems are able to utilize their RFID identification and security systems throughout internal and interlending workflows.

With coordination between RFID and ILS vendors, RFID may change the security landscape for media material that is moving between libraries. Many libraries secure media in a locking case. When such materials are shipped to other libraries, they may be placed on an unsecured shelf or be secured by keeping it behind the desk. Neither option is desirable. If all libraries in a consortium used RFID for media security, the need for locking cases would be eliminated and security would be enhanced.

The RFID tag could also carry information useful in an ILL transaction, but like delivery, using the tagged data will require coordination between RFID and ILS vendors. It is worth noting that the US data model creates an opportunity to ensure that items in transit never fall into a "black hole." Using a combination of the unique identifier and the owning library, every library item could be uniquely identified. Information about its status will be on the tag, along with information on the owning library and the borrowing library.

RFID also creates the opportunity to automatically track material. RFID tags can be used to track totes. Using longer-range RFID tags, totes could be tracked with RFID readers mounted at driver entrances. Used in combination with tote manifesting, this could provide effortless tracking of items as they move around the consortia.

The cost of RFID tags has declined over the years; however, the cost of installation and equipment is still a barrier for many small libraries. The return-on-investment time period, based on circulation and delivery labor and costs, is likely to shrink further as RFID costs continue to decrease. The success of RFID will depend heavily on the success of consortia in organizing their libraries around a specific data profile and security plan.

Other Standards

One of the challenges for resource sharing and delivery and its related technologies is the lack of standards supporting communications with the ILS. SIP2 is the de facto standard for communications with the ILS, and having this standard has been the key to making it possible to integrate third-party products into the mix of solutions libraries use to provide services. Without SIP and SIP2, the ILS vendor had a monopoly on product development. SIP provides third-party developers with limited access to ILS data.

The other protocol that is slowly being adopted is NISO Circulation Interchange Protocol (NCIP2). NCIP2 handles many of the same messages that SIP2 does, but it also handles additional messages that come into play during resource sharing. It is NCIP2 that turns a very labor-intensive ILL transaction into a one that can be largely unmediated and almost as simple as a circulation transaction from both the staff and patron point of view. NCIP is not well understood by libraries, but it holds the key to improved efficiency for libraries involved in resource-sharing consortia. A better understanding of and more support for NCIP compliance by vendors will benefit libraries and consortia.

As important as NCIP is to resource sharing, it still doesn't do all that we need it to do when it comes to resource sharing, delivery, and RFID standards. We mentioned earlier that RFID could improve delivery and sorting operations; however, the development of some of the technologies and products still rely on the ILS. And today the ILS vendors do not support the communications and message sets that would be required. Just as SIP2 opened the door for libraries to undertake self-check and other circulation functions outside of the ILS, NCIP creates the same opportunity when it comes to resource-sharing transactions. A new protocol developed in the United Kingdom has the potential to transform what third-party RFID products could do vis-à-vis the ILS. The protocol, Library Communication

Framework (LCF), was developed through a partnership of ILS and RFID vendors. It defines all the messages and data elements that are required to perform many RFID-enabled transactions (including those currently supported by SIP2). LCF is managed by Chartered Institute of Library and Information Professionals CILIP (www.cilip.org.uk).[4] The hope is that, at the very least, the LCF will inform future protocol developments that are related, including SIP2 (and SIP3), NCIP2, and any future application profiles that are developed as well as the new ISO ILL protocol currently in the works.

The standards development path is often indirect and challenging. Standards are often developed based on input that comes from committees comprised chiefly of vendors and service providers. Librarians need to be more deeply involved in standards development or at least encourage colleagues in libraries and consortia to be library-centric experts representing libraries in standards development. NISO is the library community's main provider of standards. NISO welcomes input from stakeholders in the library community, but participation in some areas is low. Without more active involvement in standards-setting bodies, these standards they develop will meet the market-based needs of vendors more than the user- or staff-oriented needs of libraries.

NISO hosts a Discovery to Delivery Topic Committee, and it provides the Discovery to Delivery Standards Portfolio at www.niso.org/topics/d2d/d2standards. The portfolio includes links to numerous protocols and information resources on the topic.

Conclusion and Consortial Implications

Academic libraries and public libraries, as well as their corresponding consortia, differ in the scale and best practices of physical delivery of library materials. Physical delivery volume is much higher in public library consortia than in academic consortia. Packaging of individual items is much more prevalent in the academic library setting. The most modern technology for materials handling is employed in larger public libraries and countywide public library systems, which have the highest levels of shipping. Consortia are not adopting materials handling systems at the consortial level.

Library customers are like all consumers. They want instant gratification. In the physical materials environment, consortia might consider employing enhanced ILS features to facilitate the quickest turnaround as well as enhanced workflows in libraries and sort sites to move requested items as quickly as possible for patron pick up. The costs for AMH systems may decline to a point that warehouse-sized systems can be justified by a reasonable return on investment period. Coordinated use of RFID and ILS communications standards should be considered. Interconsortial and/or interstate lending and delivery collaboration might also help boost service levels as well as efficiency.

The need for mass digitization of materials in the public domain is another major challenge. The DPLA and the consortia that make up its regional hubs are joined in an effort to facilitate discovery to delivery for a quickly growing number of digital items. A stable source of funding is required to support these efforts to provide open access to the hidden treasures in all of our libraries. An important question is how DPLA and its hubs can develop successful sustainability models to carry out their important work for the long term.

Notes

1. Steve Coffman, "How Low Can Our Book Budgets Go?" *American Libraries* (Sept./Oct. 2013): 50.
2. Lori Bowen Ayre, Gregory Pronevitz, and Catherine Utt, "Label-Less Library Logistics," *Collaborative Librarianship* 3, no. 3 (2011).
3. Lori Bowen Ayre, "RFID in Libraries: A Step toward Interoperability," *Library Technology Reports* 48, no. 5 (2012).
4. e4libraries, "Library Interoperability Standards," www.bic.org.uk/e4libraries/16/interoperability-standards.

Case Studies

The 16 case studies that follow explore some typical activities of consortia as well as several innovative and trendsetting projects. We invited contributors to prepare case studies to represent the wide range of activities taking place in library consortia today and to point out projects that may contribute to the sustainability of consortia. We view sustainability in two ways. First, a consortium must maintain sufficient revenue to provide services, and second, each consortium must meet its members' needs and expectations.

The 16 case studies are roughly in the order of consortial service prevalence from our survey, that is, services provided by the largest percentage of responding consortia are first. The vast majority of consortia provide training and professional development services. We asked Minitex staff to describe the organization's efforts in online instruction, which is an aspect of training that is expanding nationwide.

A large percentage of consortia provide shared electronic content. We have included several case studies that are examples of innovative new projects for providing e-content. The Enki case study, by Linda Crowe and Heather Teysko of California, describes the use of open-source software in conjunction with proprietary systems to create a system for hosting and delivering e-books published by smaller presses and other local content. The statewide e-book pilot project, by Deborah Hoadley of the Massachusetts Library System, examines several different e-book acquisition and delivery methods to determine which platforms are the best to serve all of the state's libraries.

Additional information on e-content projects follows with Mark Sullivan's (IDS Project) coverage of innovations to ensure licensing compliance for document delivery of e-journal articles in New York; Ann Okerson's (Center for Research Libraries) study on group purchasing services innovation with multiconsortial efforts of the wide deal; and Cyril Oberlander's (SUNY Geneseo) description of SUNY libraries' efforts to support authorship and editing of textbooks as well as open access to them.

We have not ignored the traditional services, however, as they are the bread and butter of most organizations. Interstate physical delivery holds promise to improve efficiency for many consortia, and Kathy Drozd (Minitex) describes the system used in Minnesota, the Dakotas, and Wisconsin to build on chapter 5's coverage of physical delivery. We have included three case studies on operating shared integrated library systems, including different outcomes in the use of open-source models. Many libraries and consortia have viewed open-source as a path to the future. We must note our disappointment that some open-source projects have deviated from their community version. The controversy with LibLime, a service provider, was described in 2010 by Marshall Breeding and, as far as we know, it continues today.[1]

Integrated library systems (ILS) are shared by more than 40 percent of our survey respondents, and we worked with three colleagues to cover that area. Randy Dykhuis (Midwest Collaborative for Library Services) provides a cautionary tale on a shared open-source Evergreen ILS. Vicki Teal Lovely (South Central Library System) shares the story of a vendor-hosted version of Koha's open-source ILS. Jeanine Gatzke and Belinda E. Lawrence (Midwest Collaborative for Library Services) provide a case study on a shared commercial ILS.

Digital and physical collections are often managed by library consortia, and we included a case study on each. The Collaborative Digital Initiatives case study by consultant Liz Bishoff examines several state-of-the-art digital libraries. Jay Schafer (University of Massachusetts-Amherst) authored a study on the shared physical repository project of the Five Colleges in western Massachusetts.

Other innovative trends related to human resources and fiscal management are detailed in the case studies. We begin with the 2CUL model in which two major universities are collaborating, sharing staffing and systems at an unprecedented level. This deep collaborative project is taking place at Cornell and Columbia Universities, and the case study was contributed by Anne R. Kenney and James Neal. The next case study in this area, by Lisa Priebe (Colorado Library Consortium), describes how a consortium can assist its partners with contracted staffing. The Bibliotemps case study, by Kelly Jo Woodside (Massachusetts Library System) examines a consortium that created a temporary employment service. Valerie Horton closes out the case studies with a picture of consortial fiscal sponsorship for projects and services at the Colorado Library Consortium.

Each case study starts with a bulleted list of the consortial or library need for the given activities. It is followed by a list of the benefits that have accrued from the service. The authors follow those lists with details about the project. It is our hope that these case studies can be used by others to push the envelope in designing successful new services.

Note

1. Marshall Breeding, "New Era for Koha: PTFS Acquires LibLime," *Library Journal* (February 2010): 15.

Online Instruction

Jennifer Hootman, Matt Lee, and Mary Parker

Need

- provide access to the Electronic Library for Minnesota (ELM) for 2,700 eligible kindergartens through high schools (K–12) and academic, public, and special libraries in Minnesota
- respond to increasing cost per on-site in-person instructional session and declining numbers of workshop attendees
- discover more cost-effective way to continue delivering high-quality ELM instruction to library and school staff at their point of need
- offer a cost-effective online option when appropriate, not replace all on-site in-person instructional sessions

Benefit

- ELM instruction via virtual conferencing software saves financial resources as well as staff time and travel expenses.
- The ability to archive sessions increases flexibility in accessing content.
- Online instruction and archives allow staff to learn about the ELM resources at their point of need.
- Through online instruction, Minitex can reach more staff of the Minnesota schools and libraries more efficiently and economically.

Minitex is a publicly supported network of academic, public, state government, and special libraries working cooperatively to improve library service for their users in Minnesota, North Dakota, and South Dakota. Minitex administers ELM, a collection of statewide electronic resources in Minnesota. A unit within Minitex called Reference Outreach & Instruction (ROI) provides and coordinates the critical instructional component for ELM that most libraries and schools cannot afford to provide on their own.

In order to provide efficient, flexible, user-friendly instruction, Minitex ROI has made online instruction a focus for a number of years. Instruction helps ensure that Minnesotans not only have access to ELM but learn how to use the resources efficiently and effectively, finding the authoritative, verifiable information they need to succeed in school or the workplace.

Minitex ROI offers a range of instruction, from live webinars to recorded webinars to small group sessions offered on demand. These varying online sessions form the backbone of our online offerings and are offered through Adobe Connect. These options allow for the flexibility Minitex needs to serve libraries of all types in all manner of environments. Offering a range of online instructional options best serves the varying learning needs of our audience.

ROI staff schedule live webinars at times that are convenient for library staff. For instance, webinars scheduled before or after typical school hours target school librarians, while sessions at midday are more likely to appeal to the public librarian's schedule. These webinars focus on practical applications of the ELM databases. In addition to detailed explorations of the ELM databases by vendor or interface, topical webinars introduce how ELM can support research into such varied endeavors as National History Day projects, science, technology, engineering and math (STEM) education, employment research, and more. Any library staff member from participating libraries can join these scheduled webinars for a quick, efficient learning experience.

Despite efforts to provide live webinars at times targeted to varying library staff schedules, it has been a challenge to find a meeting time that works for a large group. Thus, we take advantage of Adobe Connect's recording functionality. All live webinars are recorded and posted to the Minitex website, where library staff can view them at any hour of the day on any device.

ROI builds context and added value to these recorded webinars by packaging them with hands-on activities, short video tutorials, and database fact sheets in the ELM Learning Center. This allows library staff to learn at their own pace and depth by choosing online instructional options that fit their needs. Library staff might watch a recorded webinar and then follow up with hands-on activities for a chance to explore on their own. Or they might scan a one-page fact sheet on a database and then view a three-minute video demonstration of that database. Most of the content within the ELM Learning Center is downloadable and customizable. These supplemental materials can be used to support the instructional efforts of library staff throughout the state for their own patrons and students or directly by the Minnesota community.

Traditionally Minitex has sought to provide these instructional opportunities solely for library staff of participating libraries. Recently, however, Minitex ROI has expanded to include K–12 teachers. In this effort ROI has found that online instruction can simultaneously serve its outreach goals as well as its instructional goals. Invitations to online offerings are created specifically for library media specialists to share with their teachers and to host group attendance at their institution.

In addition to instruction on the ELM databases, Minitex ROI strives to help participating libraries share information with each other and to keep library staff apprised of emerging trends in the field. The unit hosts and promotes webinars given by library staff from across the region who have subject expertise on topics such as government information, chat reference services, online health and medical resources, reader's advisory, and more. We also provide regional access to teleconferences on cutting-edge topics and technology from the National Information Standards Organization (NISO) and other groups.

Like other consortia and libraries, over the past ten to twelve years Minitex has adopted several different conferencing software tools. Whether it's a subscription to PlaceWare, Horizon Wimba Live Classroom, Microsoft's LiveMeeting, or most recently, to Adobe Connect, the intent has always been the same—to facilitate online instruction, meetings, and demonstrations.

From its experience with a variety of conferencing software tools, ROI considers it essential to ask the following three questions when selecting software appropriate to the proposed intent:

1. How does it present content?
2. How does it facilitate interaction?
3. What is the learner experience?

Answers to these questions will help any institution determine the features most important to their online instruction and meeting goals.

ROI considers a high level of interactivity crucial to the online experience it wishes to provide to its audience, and it chooses its software accordingly. Chat, whiteboard tools, polling, breakout rooms, screen sharing for presenter and attendees, audio options and quality, recording and archiving capability, and ease-of-use have all been priority features. Adobe Connect, the unit's current online software tool, has met these criteria and improves the overall quality of the learner and instructor experience.

Garnering attendance and improving the effectiveness of the unit's promotional communication continue to be ongoing challenges for Minitex ROI's online instruction. These challenges are not atypical for consortia trainers. Some of the unit's efforts to grow and deepen promotional communication and contact lists have included

1. creating a web-based visual e-mail announcement template as well as combining and deduplicating e-mail lists of library staff;
2. expanding the unit's contacts to teachers, K–12 administrators, and curriculum coordinators by building relationships and forwarding the official e-mail announcements directly rather than relying on others to share that information with them; and
3. exhibiting and presenting at conferences outside the library profession to classroom teachers, faculty, administrators, and home educators.

We continue to address these challenges by continually investigating new and better ways to communicate and reach out to a complex audience.

Minitex has found that our mix of online and on-site sessions, coupled with the availability of online tutorials and archived webinars, has met the needs of our audience. As part of these broad ongoing instructional efforts, ROI is committed to maintaining and growing its online offerings. Shrinking budgets coupled with advances in online teaching and learning technology make that a practical priority. Online tools, including Adobe Connect, Google applications, and others, ensure that our instructional offerings and teaching tools are accessible, available, and easy to use.

Whether on-site or online, Minitex ROI instructional efforts directly contribute to the sustainability of Minitex. This work ensures that the Electronic Library for Minnesota, one of the core resources supported by Minitex, is understood and used more frequently. In this way, the unit's instructional work is inherently an outreach effort. As we continue to provide instructional opportunities and materials, Minitex also directly extends its services and presence not just to library staff but also to all Minnesotans. Minitex's online instruction has become a core service, and ROI provides an essential value-added service that demonstrates directly to the community that Minitex is a consortium worthy of continued financial support.

The Enki Experiment: Library E-book Consortia System

Linda Crowe and Heather Teysko

Need

- great patron demand for e-books
- desire for control over e-book collections; leasing no longer considered a viable option
- integration of materials into the library's own platform to achieve system functionality
- library staff interest in building relationships with e-book authors and publishers

Benefit

- building relationships with independent publishers and other consortia and state libraries
- gaining control of part of the e-book collections
- learning to use discovery tools to link separate library catalogs

The Califa Group has a long history of working with e-books. Since its inception we have worked with e-book providers such as NetLibrary, Ingram's MyiLibrary, Safari, Recorded Books, and OverDrive. In fact, we worked with OverDrive from 2004-2008, and our frustrations began to simmer when our contract was not renewed in 2008 and we were left without a platform for valuable consortial e-book content. We had no other acceptable options.

In 2011, EBSCO purchased NetLibrary, and Recorded Books took over MyiLibrary's e-audio product. Vendor activities like this made us boil with frustration. We felt that we were at the mercy of vendors, being forced to change course with little to no control over the collections into which we had poured time, energy, and money. Looking into the future and considering the rising popularity of e-books, this problem could only get worse.

There had to be a better way for our libraries to invest in e-books that would remain part of the library's collection. The staff needed and wanted to build lasting relationships with publishers and authors, and to integrate materials into a platform at their own speed with reliable functionality. There are some libraries that can manage e-book systems themselves, but the majority of libraries in California rely on a consortium to take them to this level.

After seeing the model that Douglas County, Colorado, had built, we decided to build a Califa e-book platform. At the time we had no idea what that meant. We just knew that we wanted to be a part of developing library-based solutions. We weren't sure what our platform would look like—whether it would be a shared collection, who would work with us, or how we would even build it. We also knew that being part of a solution meant getting to work. We immediately started to research, talk with publishers, and find technical developers.

The outpouring of support from member libraries, other organizations, publishers, and technology groups was overwhelming. Everyone wanted to help us build an e-book solution. Having a very small staff has allowed Califa to be nimble and act quickly, but not having a full-time technical team meant that we couldn't do this project on our own. We needed a technology partner. Contra Costa County, a member library known for its technical skills and innovation, was willing to partner with us to build an e-book platform. Contra Costa contracts with the Quipu Group, a technology group of librarians based in Colorado, and from those contacts a core team was developed with the three organizations. We decided to name the project Enki, which comes from the name of a Sumerian deity of mischief, intelligence, and creativity, We think it accurately represents our project.

In the most simplistic terms, there are only a few things a library needs to build an e-book platform:

- a place to store the files
- a way to add Digital Rights Management (DRM)
- a way for users to search for books
- a way for users to check them out

Of course, it is critical that those components connect to each other. There are many steps in each of these broad categories, but these four points provide a way to break down the necessary technology.

Storing the files is simply hosting—having either a server on site or a remote cloud-based server where we could keep e-book files. We spent four months researching the best hosting options because we wanted a system that could easily scale up as this project grew. We decided on a vendor-based cloud solution from hosting.com, and we have been happy with their service.

The Digital Rights Management (DRM) is handled by the Adobe Content Server (ACS), a piece of software that is now the industry-standard for adding DRM. Most publishers are comfortable working with ACS. The cost for the ACS in 2013 was a one-time fee of $10,000 with an additional $1,500/year in maintenance. We will also pay $.08 every time someone checks out a book.

For the discovery layer, we decided to go with VuFind+, an open-access tool. VuFind+ is a version of the software that was developed by the MARMOT Library Network in Colorado, and it includes features that are designed for consortia. The discovery layer and patron authentication portions have proved to be the most difficult for us because the VuFind system was designed to work with a single integrated library system (ILS). Since we are building a shared collection, we needed to be able to authenticate our shared collection across multiple ILS systems. There was a great deal of original programming that went into creating the discovery layer, and the next phase of development will allow for libraries to purchase locally owned content in addition to participating in the shared collection.

Califa's strength is in negotiations and purchasing, so we took on the role of negotiating with publishers. To start building publisher relationships, we attended the National BookExpo Association conference in New York, the largest publishing conference in the country. We were surprised at how many independent publishers were anxious to work with us. Many of them feel that they are sidelined by the big reseller vendors and are excited to have a way to connect with libraries directly. So far we have limited our efforts to the independent publishers, because they are the ones who were willing to take a chance and try this new model. Just as importantly, they want to work with libraries and have much the same mission, which is growing readership of their titles rather than a focusing on shareholder value. Our collection as of September 2013 has approximately 10,000 titles.

We launched in beta with Contra Costa County using CARL.X ILS in May 2013, followed by other BALIS libraries in the Bay Area that use Innovative Interfaces ILS. This beta launch will test the strength of the patron authentication system against various ILS systems. The State Library of Kansas, which joined our efforts early in the process by contributing seed money, was also authenticated on the Enki platform over the summer, and it will be followed in the fall of 2014 by libraries in the Pacific Library Partnership, a consortium of California libraries from Monterey to Marin counties.

With little marketing, some libraries are already showing more checkouts from Enki than from other vendor e-book products. When all our beta launches are complete, time will be spent testing and gathering statistics before introducing a final version to our member libraries. A complete list of participating libraries can be seen by clicking on the "choose your library" drop-down menu at www.enkilibrary.org. Although it has been a lot of hard work, with twists and turns that Califa never anticipated, the final outcome will be libraries lending consortium-owned materials on a consortium-owned platform. We believe the end product will certainly be worth the effort.

Statewide E-book Project for Multitype Libraries in Massachusetts

Deborah Hoadley

Need

- Patron demand for e-books has increased substantially over the past two years in a rapidly changing e-book environment.
- Libraries of all types want e-books at a price they can afford to meet the demands of their patrons.
- Centralized technology management, contract negotiations, and support/training services are needed for e-books.
- A flexible partner organization that could quickly develop a process to research, implement, and evaluate a statewide e-book pilot project.

Benefit

- All library card holders in Massachusetts have access to a broad selection of titles through a single user-friendly, state-wide discovery platform.
- Libraries will participate in building a statewide shared e-book collection.

- Ownership, leasing options, short-term loans, and subscription e-book models are explored.
- Opportunities are available to contribute to and provide an entrée to local content, such as history, literature, and news.

In May 2012, the Massachusetts Library System (MLS) and the Massachusetts Board of Library Commissioners (MBLC) hosted an event entitled "Resource Sharing Unbound." This event featured two keynote speakers, James G. Neal, vice president for Information Services and university librarian at Columbia University, and James LaRue, director, Douglas County Libraries in Colorado. A discussion among MLS members was facilitated at the end of the day to determine and prioritize which statewide initiatives libraries should investigate further. Three priorities were identified:

- developing a statewide library card
- implementing a statewide discovery solution
- creating a statewide e-book platform with shared content that is integrated into library catalogs

A Statewide Resource Sharing Committee (SRSC) was appointed by the MBLC to look into these initiatives. This committee heard the members' call to action at the conference, and in October 2012, a business plan for a statewide e-book project was written that outlined the scope, proof-of-concept, timeline, and possible funding model for future sustainability.

The benefits of this project include the ability to explore a variety of e-book models, including ownership, leasing, short-term loans, and subscription models. Each of these models typically fit a specific library type, such as the subscription model that is used primarily by academic libraries. A drawback is that not all publishers have the same permissions and licensing agreements with the e-book vendors, and each publisher agreement will have to be negotiated individually to allow statewide consortial agreements. This is a serious problem in the world of e-books. The American Library Association (ALA) and other organizations are trying to address the rights and access to e-books and are searching for ways to make them equitable in price and access to their print counterpart.

In late fall 2012, members of the SRSC met with libraries who might be interested in being part of the pilot project. The SRSC was also developing an information session and discussion document to share with libraries. The purpose of the document was to facilitate discussion around the challenges and benefits of and budgeting issues related to the current e-book environment, and how the statewide e-book project would be shaped.

As a sidenote, very early on in the discussions, the Douglas County Model was the preferred method for launching this e-book project. The Douglas County Model includes purchasing and licensing an Adobe Content Server, creating a technological infrastructure to access the e-books using VUFind+, and also negotiating with publishers to purchase titles. Due to the tight timeline, the technological challenges of self-hosting, and the required system development, the Douglas County Model was no longer considered a viable choice. However, in the future it is possible that Massachusetts will consider developing a statewide option very similar to the Douglas County Model. Currently, there are a number of states, including Kansas and California (See Case Study 2, The Enki Experiment), that are adopting the Douglas County Model.

In late December 2012, it was determined that MLS would be the organization to manage the statewide e-book project because it was prepared to develop the project quickly. The SRSC identified many steps necessary to execute this project. The first step was to meet and discuss the aspects of the pilot project with affiliated library groups across the state. The reason for this discussion was to garner statewide support from the various stakeholders and partners, to broaden the scope of what libraries wanted, and to begin setting reasonable expectations for the pilot project.

The second step was to identify the 50 pilot libraries. We wanted all types of libraries (academic, public, school, and special) represented. The breakdown of libraries was to be: 25 public, 10 academic, 10 school, and 5 special libraries. We also wanted to include libraries from each of the ten automated networks in the state and balance size, population, and location of the libraries across the pilot project. Many libraries were interested immediately, and five of the interested libraries became known as the alpha libraries. These alpha libraries were responsible to recruit nine other libraries according to the criteria. It turned out to be easy to identify additional libraries, with the exception of the special libraries. They were harder to recruit, and in the end only two special libraries participated in the pilot project. As we move forward with the project, special attention will be given to evaluating the relevancy of the collection for special libraries.

This pilot project will be funded through a grant from MBLC and monies from MLS dedicated to online content for member libraries. The total amount needed is $400,000–$600,000, which is expected to fund the pilot project for 6–12 months. After the pilot project, libraries will be asked to fund future e-book content. MLS and MBLC plan to provide support to maintain the infrastructure, including technological needs, negotiations with companies and publishers, training and support for member libraries and other operational aspects such as billing and dedicated staff.

This project had a very aggressive timeline. The Request for Proposal (RFP) was originally slated to be issued in November or December 2012, with an ending date for the pilot set at December 31, 2013. These deadlines were not realistic, as MLS was only brought on as project manager in late December, and more groundwork for the project had to be laid before moving into the RFP phase. A transition of the project from the different working groups within the SRSC also took some time. However, we realized that the rapidly changing e-book environment necessitated an aggressive timeline, and we still wanted to have the project started by fall 2013.

The RFP for an e-book content platform and e-book content was issued in March 2013, and a deadline for submissions was set for April. Through this RFP we wanted to learn which vendors had distinctive platforms providing access to the e-book content, and also which vendors could provide e-book content that would serve all the collection development needs of the multitype libraries.

The main components of the RFP included

- description and background of the project;
- critical success factors for 50 pilot libraries and a gradual statewide rollout;
- goals;
- definitions and special issues;
- submission procedures;
- proposed pricing and billing conditions; and
- an evaluation criteria checklist.

A separate section of the RFP focused on particular specifications. These were

- discovery,
- ILS integration and interoperability,

- publishing/repository,
- rights, permissions & licensing,
- accessibility,
- reports, and
- training & implementation.

Also included with the RFP was a ReadersFirst content access requirements document, *ALA's EBook Business Models: A Scorecard for Public Libraries* (www.districtdispatch.org/wp-content/uploads/2013/01/Ebook_Scorecard .pdf) and a list of the 50 pilot library names.

We received 13 vendor responses. Most of the vendors submitted responses for both an e-book content platform and actual content. Vendors submitting a response for e-book content only were too limited in their collection to be viable. These limits were related to licensing and publisher restrictions.

Before the RFP was issued, we decided to consider including more than one vendor for the pilot project. Vendors were selected according to the score they received from a comprehensive rubric based on the different components from the RFP. Only vendors receiving a high score—7 of the 13 vendors—were asked to participate in vendor demonstrations. Approximately 30 people attended the presentations in person or online. Each presentation was recorded for future viewing by the pilot libraries. Along with the recording, each vendor also provided trial access to their products.

Three vendors were chosen for the pilot project. These vendors met three priorities. First, and most importantly, the interface and end-user experience was easy to navigate. Second, each vendor offered a different model of e-book access, allowing us to explore different options for delivering e-books, including purchasing and owning titles, subscribing to a collection of titles and allowing short-term loans, and uploading and curating local content either from authors or digitized projects from libraries. A pilot project goal was to have 10,000 titles as an opening collection. This goal could only be accomplished by having three vendors offer different e-book delivery models.

Our third priority was for the vendor to have prior experience working with libraries and working on other e-book projects. We needed to have companies willing to work through this project with an open mind and entrepreneurial spirit. The companies also had to have a plan to phase-in the remainder of the approximately 1,600 MLS member libraries into their e-book system over a two-year period once the pilot project was completed.

As this case study is being written, MLS is in the negotiation phase of the terms and conditions based on the scope of the project. We face the challenge of working with vendors who only had experience with single libraries, not consortia. Publisher restrictions limit the amount of content MLS can potentially purchase until new license negotiations can be worked out between the companies and publishers. MLS created a terms and conditions agreement covering the initial goals of the project. These contracts will need to be revisited as MLS works with more vendors to provide additional content and platforms in the future.

To deal with the complexity of communications, sustainability, training programs, and evaluation, three task forces were established. Each pilot library had the opportunity to participate. These task forces are: Statewide Collection Development & Collection Development Policy group, Promotion & Training group, Sustainability & Funding group.

Each task force has representatives from the various types, sizes, and locations of Massachusetts' libraries. Representatives from the SRSC, MBLC, and MLS are also part of each task force. We expect these groups to continue beyond the pilot project and to be part of the permanent infrastructure of the Massachusetts E-book Project. Another aspect of this project will be to create an evaluation and assessment for library staff and patrons. Additional resources have been developed to help promote this project to the broader library community including a website (http://guides .masslibsystem.org/ebookproject).

While this pilot project is still in its infancy, there is great hope for successful collaboration between the different statewide organizations, MLS member libraries, vendors, and publishers. We know there will be challenges and successes along the way. Inclusion of e-books will continue to be an integral part of library collections, and rapid progress is being made nationwide in creating affordable models. Libraries must embrace new models and continue their quest to reduce the threat to resource sharing, which is so critical to the future of all libraries. This e-book project is one way to break down the barriers to access and push the boundaries that currently exist in the e-book environment.

Article Licensing Information Availability Service (ALIAS)

Mark Sullivan

Need

- identify the journal holdings in databases from member libraries
- create easy access to licensing information for journals in member databases
- double the fill rate for resource-sharing article requests within Information Delivery Services Project (IDS)

Benefit

- decrease turnaround time of article requests for patrons
- reduce workload by automating the processing required at the borrowing library
- reduce costs by decreasing the number of requests that go to libraries that charge fees

ALIAS is a system that was nearly ten years in the making, and it is now in use by 70 IDS Project libraries. The IDS Project was conceived by Edwin Rivenburgh, then director of Milne Library at SUNY Geneseo, and it was backed by eleven other New York State academic library directors. These directors believed that to survive and prosper in the twenty-first century, libraries would need to radically change the way they do business with each other. Towards this goal, the IDS Project was developed to advance the sharing of library resources through collaboration, innovation, and efficiency.

Members commit to meeting delivery goals based on a user-centric definition of an interlibrary loan transaction: from the time the user places a request until the time the user is notified the loan is ready for pickup or is ready to be retrieved from the Web. The IDS standards for delivery are 48 hours for articles and 72 hours for loans. To date, the IDS Project has over 70 member academic, special, and public libraries, including the New York State Library and the New York Public Library.

In the fall of 2004, soon after the IDS Project began, we ran a newly developed statistic system to determine the transaction times and fill rate within the member libraries. While the overall statistics showed that we had a lot of work to do to meet the delivery standards, the results were very promising. However, the fill rate for articles within the project was exceedingly low, and it seemed impossible that we were filling less than 33 percent of the article requests considering the large amount of money each library was spending on journals. All member libraries were using ILLiad and OCLC for resource-sharing management, which worked extremely well for monographs and print journals. The problem was that none of the libraries were loading holdings information for electronic journals into OCLC. In their defense, there wasn't a good way to do this.

To test the theory that we could fill a much larger number of article requests with electronic journals, we cobbled together a web-based search system that ran independent searches of each library's OpenURL resolvers, which contained their journal holdings data. The results were dramatic and showed that we could fill another 31 percent of article requests from within the project if we could discover what each member held—and if we could determine the licenses for each one. In 2005, SUNY switched from Ex Libris's SFX to Serials Solutions, which simplified the process of extracting holdings data because all of the other non-SUNY IDS libraries were using Serials Solutions.

After several months of unsuccessfully searching for an electronic rights management system that would suit our needs and have some general licensing data already loaded, we built our own. Data was downloaded from Serials Solutions and loaded into an Index Data Zebra z39.50 index server. The staff members at the project libraries were able to connect to our newly created eJournal Availability Server using the ILLiad client and to run searches on the ISSNs of the journals. The first stage of development was never implemented on a project-wide scale, however, because no one was comfortable loaning articles without knowing that the contracts allowed it.

The second stage involved obtaining license and contract information for the interlibrary loan (ILL) rights of each electronic journal. Instead of using the traditional "What did you sign at your library?" we decided to see what each publisher and aggregator was displaying on their websites. General terms of service, user rights, and licensing data were collected from the websites of nearly all publishers and providers. Publishers that didn't have information published on their websites were sent e-mails requesting their general contract language. Interestingly, several responded that they had not considered ILL rights for e-journals and asked if we would provide language for them to include. The language we provided was the equivalent of Fair Use Rights. It took several months to compile the licensing data and to integrate it with the holdings data. The first step of discoverability and license availability was completed, but it was done manually, which was slow.

In 2008, the IDS Project began working with Atlas Systems, the creators of ILLiad, to produce an improved version of the existing e-journal availability. This new version would have several components:

1. Similar holdings and license database
2. A load-balancing web service that would spread the requests among all of the members
3. An ILLiad server-side Microsoft Windows service that would allow for automatic request processing based on the holdings, license, and load-balancing data.

Together, these three pieces would form the Article Licensing Information Availability Service (ALIAS). The IDS Service and load-balancing system that Atlas System's created took our data system and turned it into a fully unmediated article request system.

ALIAS was beta tested during the spring of 2008 with six libraries and brought online for all IDS libraries after the August 2008 IDS Project Conference. One of the most immediately noticeable results of the unmediated service was the decrease in time between receiving a patron's article request and sending the request to OCLC. Prior to ALIAS, it was not uncommon for a request to sit in queue for several hours or even more than a day. During the initial beta period of ALIAS, some of the libraries were able to demonstrate the improvement by reducing the average time from more than a day to an average of approximately two hours for the entire request. The data also showed that even with the amount of effort put into ALIAS, only 54 percent of the requests submitted could be processed automatically. We found that

- 44 percent of requests were sent to OCLC and then on to the first library in the ALIAS-generated lender string;
- 10 percent were determined to be held locally and were routed to a local holdings queue; and
- the remaining 46 percent were handled manually. The IDS Service placed a note in each request explaining why ALIAS was unable to process the request.

The majority of nonlicensing issues were due to a lack of an ISSN in the request. The remaining issues either involved a license that didn't allow for loans or no record of the journal being available at any of the IDS libraries. Considering that only six libraries were involved with the beta test, we hoped that this number would decrease substantially once the rest of the libraries were brought online.

The data from January 2013 to May 2013 has shown that 50 percent of over 60,000 article requests were handled successfully by ALIAS and another 19 percent were handled manually and sent to other IDS member libraries. The initial issue was why the 19 percent failed to be processed automatically. The primary reason was that patrons were submitting invalid ISSNs. Over 9,000 of the unsuccessful requests had invalid data, including an apology in the ISSN field for not having the proper ISSN. Better discovery tools and user education would help reduce this number substantially.

The remaining 31 percent of the requests that required going to libraries outside of the IDS Project were due to a lack of holdings. However, it wasn't that the member libraries didn't have the required journals; they didn't have access to the required issues. The electronic journal embargo periods and lack of digitization of older volumes prevented the member libraries from filling over 8,000 requests (13%) during the first half of 2013. If the embargo period was removed so that e-journals were treated like their print counterparts, 82 percent of the requests would have been filled. The remaining 18 percent would still need to be filled by libraries outside of the IDS Project or through purchase elsewhere.

The ALIAS license data is updated each year by a team of 20 or more librarians from across the IDS Project libraries. However, spring 2013 marked the first time in years that the interface to the ALIAS database was updated. A joint librarian, faculty, and student team at SUNY Sullivan created a new interface that should speed up the processing of the licenses dramatically.

In the next few months, the IDS Project will begin work on ALIAS 2.0. This new version is based upon ILLiad 8.4 and the server-side Addons that were made available in version 8.3. ALIAS 2.0 will begin with the conversion of the IDS service from a Windows service into an ILLiad server-side Addon. This change will

- allow easier installs and updates,
- allow for easier searching of Serials Solutions/SFX for missing ISSNs, and
- no longer require Atlas to install the Windows service onto the OCLC host servers or campus information technology departments to install it onto local servers.

ALIAS 2.0 is currently under development.

The IDS Project is committed to providing improvements to the entire resource-sharing community through the ongoing development and sharing of innovative tools and promotion of best practices. ALIAS, although primarily a system for IDS Project Libraries, has also had an effect on outside libraries through the freely accessible Serials Solutions and SFX Addons. ALIAS also provided the model for OCLC's Direct Request for Articles, which is now in its third year of operation.[1] The IDS Project will continue to work with Atlas Systems and OCLC to improve workflow and to create new tools for the resource-sharing community.

Note

1. "OCLC, IDS Project and Atlas Systems to Develop Network-level Solution for Unmediated Article Resource Sharing," http://worldcat.org/arcviewer/1/OCC/2011/11/08/H1320767091756/viewer/file4022.htm.

Embracing Wide Deals (Interconsortial Licensing)

Ann Okerson

Need

- respond to user demand for more journal and e-resource content even as library budgets are severely restrained
- streamline labor-intensive e-content licensing
- create more transparency and consistency in e-resource pricing and terms

Benefit

- leverage the buying power of a large number of libraries
- develop more coordination, efficiency, and transparency with advantageous prices and user terms

There's really nothing new about library consortia; the oldest go back decades. There's really nothing new about licensing electronic resources either; again, the first inklings are decades old. But licensing large amounts of what we now cold-bloodedly call content in order to make that content available to users, and doing so through sophisticated consortia led by canny and experienced leaders—that is something we learned to do only in the 1980s and 1990s.

111

But times are changing rapidly nowadays. An emerging trend that deserves to be noticed, understood, and interpreted is the growth of what I have called the wide deal. Others have called these interconsortial licensing or ICL for short. Wide deal is a play on words, alluding to the everyday phrase the Big Deal. The Big Deal is another invention of the 1990s, referring to the kind of arrangement in which a library or consortium takes a single large package of content from a given publisher for a single price. The Big Deal usually features far more content than that library or those libraries would have subscribed to before, for about the same price. For our purposes here we can leave to the side the arguments about the wisdom and future of the Big Deal. In this case study, I will concentrate on the dimension of magnitude.

A wide deal embraces several or many consortia working together on the behalf of the reader. Such a wide deal can be a big deal (a large package of content) or not (it could focus on a single significant resource). What is different today is the way groups of consortia are growing interested in working together for the benefit of their collective users. The assumption here is that such an interconsortial deal, if it is the shape of things to come, offers a path forward to broadening or universalizing access to particular kinds of resources.

Why would consortia enter into such arrangements? What are the advantages they bring? When wide deals capture a very broad swath of libraries, they can leverage the buying power of a large number of libraries at once. In principle, the more participants there are, the better the deal should be. In times of restricted funding for libraries, that means better financial and use terms, as well as more content for the same spend. As negotiating strategy, it means that publishers may have less opportunity to divide and conquer in a series of one-off deals with individual institutions. These deals are often hedged with nondisclosure requirements.

Wide deals increase the overall effectiveness and efficiency of licensing, using fewer but more experienced people to license the same resources. This concentration of libraries' buying power and talent can more effectively get the attention of publishers. Dealing wide is an approach that can strengthen a negotiator's hands sufficiently to be a game changer. Obviously, this kind of arrangement works only when publishers are willing to see the benefits for themselves: efficiency and potential access to many more readers at once.

Librarians and publishers all know why licensing cooperation is important. To succeed now requires more of the following:

- Advocacy: consortia need to make libraries' needs and capacities understood to publishers and constituents
- Productivity: with more consortia engaged on a given deal, there is the potential for getting more content for a better price with less overhead
- Elevation: better deals can attract more participating libraries to take up the offer, thus benefitting more users and saving more money
- Coordination and synchronization: achieved through working together on common resources at common times, more efficiently, more rapidly, and with better outcomes

The emerging wide deals should have some important common characteristics. First, negotiators must consistently secure the very best arrangement possible. That best is defined as something better than the publisher offered at the outset or that could be achieved by an individual library or consortium. For example, offers can involve sliding pricing that lead to good-better-best results. With such offers, libraries exploit the communications network among consortia to best effect while responding to publisher marketing in a timely way that benefits both sides. Consortial administrative capacities are also exploited to best effect.

These types of cross-consortia deals may be regional, national, or international. Their scope is continually expanding. Starting in the late 1990s, the International Coalition of Library Consortia (ICOLC) has been the main forum for talking shop and a leader in consortial dealing worldwide.[1] In the late 1990s through ICOLC, US consortia achieved a common license for the large aggregated electronic resource *Academic Universe*.[2] That deal is the oldest and the still-standing equivalent of a national site license in the United States. Meanwhile, WALDO in New York, licensing for no fewer than 900 member institutions, brings together individual institutions and consortia and works with dozens of publishers.[3] At the same time, LYRASIS has evolved into a powerhouse with over 1,700 member institutions and offers services to many more. LYRASIS includes other consortia among those that it represents. In addition to licensing for its members, it has negotiated with certain publishers for cross-consortia deals.

For example, a video publisher has offered via LYRASIS a multiconsortia arrangement, with ever-larger discounts as the library group grows. The discount tiers they recognize are participants in the following ranges: 2–5, 6–10, 11–30, 31–99, and 100+. Through the work of LYRASIS, there are growing numbers of participants, all benefitting from making it into the penultimate tier. With more time and effort, the 100+ tier is a distinct possibility for the future. This video publisher exemplifies a newer player in the e-publishing market.

Project Muse, a classic in e-journals, has newly come into e-book space. It offered, via LYRASIS/ARL, an introductory e-book deal in fall 2011, with pricing based on global uptake. As of spring 2012, the initial offer morphed into a simpler structure, with tiers of price reductions for large or very large customers. Discussions are fluid and continuing, but it is clear that Project Muse and its library customers will benefit from this scale of conversation.

If LYRASIS was doing previews of coming attractions, it would point to the recently concluded arrangement with Oxford University Press for its OUP Scholarship Online e-books. I predict that discussions will soon bear fruit with several other e-book publishers—all offers with sliding-scale discounts. Several further e-resource deals with potential interconsortial components are under investigation or in process.

There also has been a modest emerging wave of cross-national deals. For example, in a pilot some five years ago, Knowledge Exchange Project (Germany, Netherlands, Denmark, UK) issued multinational tenders for resources.[4] The project is dormant but slated to resume in the future, perhaps with a different configuration of nations. Europeans are pursuing other cross-country arrangements at this time.

At the Center for Research Libraries (CRL), we have been piloting cross-national and cross-consortial approaches. We realize that for the best arrangements, even our 270 members are not always enough for the best terms—particularly for specialist resources in which only a small fraction of the large membership will have research interests.[5] CRL has started to work with international partners in the Canadian Research Knowledge Network (CRKN-Canada), JISC-UK, and with a group of US consortia called CRL-Friends.[6] These are groups with overlapping library members. Some of the pilot projects we have worked on include:

- *19th Century Collections Online* (NCCO) Gale-Cengage. For the first four modules, we received an aggressive publisher offer of up to 55 percent discount. This arrangement brought together CRL, CRL-Friends, and CRKN in a single negotiation and contract. Their new offer for modules 5–8 includes the Australian and New Zealand consortia. The project has been well received and has attracted the same high level of participation.

- The *Churchill Archive* (CA) from Bloomsbury UK, a vast collection of materials from the papers of Winston Churchill, brought an offer of up to 30 percent discount, depending on the exact level of uptake achieved. For this resource, CRL worked with CRKN, JISC, and CRL-Friends in a first round.

Both of these projects looked to deliver new products with higher demand and high-quality functionalities. Both publishers were open to cross-consortial arrangements and good licensing terms from the library point of view. Vendor communications have been excellent, and the vendors did a great deal of work to bring the deals together. CRL has also offered a modest number of other wide historical/archival database deals to partners. Of course these are only first fruits and first steps. As interconsortial arrangements move forward, there are some important questions to keep in mind and resolve.

What is the appropriate scale for licensing these projects? At CRL, we look at this question first with respect to the resources being licensed: single resources, subsets of a publisher's output, or for large swaths of a publisher's product. Next we need to approach the right sets of users, ranging from CRL's area programs, to all CRL members, to CRL plus selected partners, and perhaps to CRL with partners in large consortia, overlapping and otherwise.

Larger questions include:

- How do consortia that offer deals not only to their own members but also to other consortia assure and manage member benefits?
- What is the best way to collaborate with partner consortia? That question can be a particular challenge in getting the best offer to be workable across national boundaries.

- Administratively, how to increase capacity for doing the work of contracting for e-resources in a new way?

All who offer wide deals need to pay attention to workflows, to the redirection and rationalization of duties, and to provision of additional support.

We also need to consider what will be the best library payment mechanisms in varying circumstances. For example, when does it make sense to have individual libraries or consortia pay the publisher directly and when does it make sense to aggregate the dollars to a single payer? And a consortium needs to be careful not to undermine its own privilege-of-membership benefits, particularly when the consortium is supported by member dues. In such a case, it will likely be necessary to charge nonmembers a small handling fee or a percentage to pay for services and negotiations.

A final and yet unresolved question for wide deal efforts is how to clarify which group will pursue which e-resources on behalf of the cross-consortial partners. The answer requires an articulated clarity of mission by each consortium so that unnecessary muddle, time-sinks, or inadvertent competition are avoided. Finally, e-resources, especially large databases in support of research, tend to be very costly. Member libraries need sufficient lead time to evaluate such resources, and where they are of interest, libraries need sufficient time to identify and allocate funds for these purchases. Thus cross-consortial wide deal licensing involves thoughtful activities in filling the pipeline, so that each deal offers the best possible advance information and has the greatest chance of uptake. Discussions about these challenges for broad collaboration are in their early stages. Proponents of this type of cooperation believe that experience to date is most promising and that a growing number of libraries—and particularly their students and researchers—will benefit.

Notes

1. The International Coalition of Library Consortia. http://en.wikipedia.org/wiki/International_Coalition_of_Library_Consortia.
2. For a description, see www.lyrasis.org/About-Us.aspx.
3. The Westchester Academic Library Directors Organization, www.waldolib.org/members.asp.
4. Wilma Mossink and Max Vogler, "Knowledge Exchange Multinational Licensing Tender: An Evaluation," *Serials: The Journal for the Serials Community* 21 (March 2008): 19–24.

5. For detailed information about the Center and its work, see www.crl.org.
6. Center for Research Libraries, "CRL Working with CRKN, JISC," www.crl.edu/news/7582.

Open SUNY Textbook Program

Cyril Oberlander

Need

- Students are unable to afford the high cost of textbooks, and this often detrimentally impacts their studies.
- Providing textbooks to students is often prohibitively expensive and difficult for libraries.
- Expanding the library's role in student learning on campus will benefit all students.

Benefit

- Enables libraries and faculty to produce high-quality open textbooks.
- Reduces the cost barriers to education and support faculty authorship.
- Builds a collaborative framework and innovative partnership of faculty, librarians, and instructional designers.
- Raises the global impact of teaching and learning.

State University of New York (SUNY) libraries have been addressing the rising cost of textbooks for years. Each library has developed distinct and independent strategies for dealing with textbook costs and the resulting impact on our students. Recently, however, SUNY libraries started taking the initiative to explore collaborative strategies and solutions that will reduce textbook costs. One group of libraries has adopted a publisher subscription model that licenses online textbooks from commercial publishers, while another group has developed a pilot program to create open textbooks. This later program is known as the Open SUNY Textbook project.

In the past, the most common strategy for academic libraries to address textbook costs has been to place textbooks on course reserves. However, academic libraries managing textbooks on reserve face several challenges, among them:

- Funding the purchase of textbooks is costly, and libraries are generally unable to provide all the required readings.
- Short checkout periods for high-use textbooks give libraries a limited capacity to adequately and reliably serve the needs of students.
- Circulating high-use textbooks from shelves behind the counter and administering overdue fines takes staff time away from other essential duties and therefore is costly in terms of library staffing.

Maintaining library textbooks on reserve is clearly a limited, expensive, and unsustainable solution. Academic libraries and their academic institutions need new strategies that reduce the cost of textbooks. Innovative strategies are essential because the cost of textbooks has a direct and measurable impact on learning. In a study of over 22,000 students, the *2012 Florida Student Textbook Survey* found that because of textbook costs, at times 64 percent of students didn't purchase a required textbook, 45 percent did not register for a course, 49 percent took fewer courses, and 27 percent dropped a course.[1] In addition, between 2002 and 2012, during a severe economic recession, the cost of textbooks rose 82 percent, as reported by the 2013 U.S. GAO report *College Textbooks*.[2] The average annual cost of textbooks, according to the College Board, is $1,200 per year.

If the Open SUNY Textbook program could reduce that average cost by only 10 percent, in the next few years, the annual cost savings to our

462,698 SUNY students could be over $5.5 million. The projected cost savings would increase with the number of titles that are published and adopted, as well as any expanded use beyond SUNY.

The Open SUNY Textbook program is a new strategy to create a publishing initiative designed to lower the cost of textbooks, raise the global impact of teaching and learning through high-quality free learning resources, and enhance the connections between author and reader. The goal is to make this program both a scalable and a sustainable solution to lowering the cost of textbooks. In order to achieve these goals, collaboration is essential. In essence SUNY libraries are leading a publishing program that is a collaboration between faculty authors, reviewers, and librarians, all solving real-world problems with innovation. Together, we can significantly and positively impact higher education while reducing cost barriers to students and highlighting faculty authorship.

Origins of the Pilot

In 2012, SUNY announced an Innovative Instruction Technology Grants program (IITG) establishing a competitive peer-reviewed award of up to $60,000 to "demonstrate, communicate and replicate innovations developed at the campus (departmental) level throughout SUNY."[3] Cyril Oberlander, SUNY Geneseo's Milne Library director and principal investigator, wrote a grant application for $20,000 in collaboration with librarians from Geneseo, The College at Brockport, The College of Environmental Science and Forestry, Upstate Medical University, and University at Buffalo. These participating libraries, along with SUNY Fredonia which joined later, piloted the publication and development of this unique open textbook program. Open textbooks are free or freely-distributed online textbooks that help reduce the cost barriers to education. Open textbooks are available using a Creative Commons license (CC-BY-NC-SA) that allows everyone to read online free of charge and print, copy, or adapt with attribution for noncommercial purposes and derivatives that are shared-alike.

The primary goals of the Open SUNY Textbook grant application were to establish a pilot for reducing cost barriers to higher education and to develop a distributed library publishing service infrastructure. The grant was also designed to encourage innovation and collaboration across higher education institutions. Ideally the Open SUNY Textbook program develops a community of practice among libraries that encourages faculty authorship and the growth of academic-friendly publishing services.

Fortunately, this unique program was awarded IITG funding in July 2012, and the participants began building a collaborative framework and innovative partnership of faculty, librarians, and instructional designers. SUNY Press also joined the program as a publishing consultant. Donna Dixon, co-director of SUNY Press, described the editorial workflow and shared templates they utilize for publishing scholarly monographs. The Open SUNY textbook publishing program is not a university press; it is an evolving publishing service created to serve a niche need. Nevertheless, the SUNY Press templates and advice served to help frame our thinking and guide the design of various forms (acceptance, revise and resubmit, reviewer letters) and to develop manuscript style guides. Details about the Open SUNY Textbook program and its templates are described in the e-book *Open SUNY Textbook Program* (http://opensuny.org/omp/index.php/SUNYOpenTextbooks/catalog/book/9).

The Open SUNY Textbook team first wrote a call for authors and developed a rubric to evaluate any manuscript proposals received. They sent out the call for authors to all SUNY campuses, offering an incentive of $3,000 for authoring an Open SUNY Textbook or $4,000 for authoring an Open SUNY Textbook that included students in the production and assessment of their learning. Two weeks after the call for authors was sent to all SUNY campuses, the team received 38 manuscript proposals.

The $20,000 grant funding limited our selection to only four titles; however, the College of Brockport, SUNY ESF, SUNY Fredonia, and SUNY Geneseo libraries all contributed library funding to significantly increase the number of titles selected for publication from 4 to 15. This increase added a great variety of disciplines to this publishing pilot, helping the team develop a comprehensive understanding of publishing across disciplines. However, it also significantly increased the publishing challenges because we had to incorporate a variety of style guidelines, formats, and copy-editing domain expertise. That said, this was a pilot to develop distributed publishing expertise capable of scale across the academy, and the Open SUNY Textbook team and libraries were up for the challenge.

Many open textbook programs lack publishing services, including peer-review, copyediting, and text layout, that are vital for producing high-quality textbooks. These services are essential for both the faculty as authors and the faculty as textbook adopters. Open SUNY Textbooks authors receive feedback and suggestions for their textbook from a peer reviewer. The peer reviewer also provides a public review to summarize the strengths and design of the textbook for faculty considering the adoption of the textbook. These public reviews are published inside the textbook so that it follows any copies that are saved or shared. After the authors accept or reject suggestions from the reviewer and revise their manuscripts, the manuscript is copyedited by qualified librarians or professional freelance copy editors. After the author approves suggestions made by copy editors and checks the galley proof made during the text layout phase, the publishing team at SUNY Geneseo library adds the open textbook into the Open SUNY Textbook Catalog (http://opensuny.org). The works are initially published in a PDF e-book but will later be published in EPUB3 format as well to make them more accessible by a variety of mobile devices. These books are also added to OCLC's WorldCat so everyone can find them and they may also be added to the University of Minnesota's *Open Textbook Catalog*.

One of the important components being developed during the textbook pilot is a distributed pool of library publishing experts—copy editors with identified disciplinary strengths, instructional designers, graphic and text designers, and so on. The availability and accessibility of publishing experts will empower college and university faculty to publish their works. The perceived value of librarians is enhanced among faculty because they bring innovative collaborations to the learning environment in this academic-friendly model. Consortia strengthen the ability of libraries to develop publishing by taking advantage of the unique skills and individual capacity at multiple libraries. A consortial approach allows the project to expand or contract more easily and operate more cost effectively.

Open SUNY Textbooks are freely available to everyone thanks to the authors and their use of a Creative Commons License, Attribution-Non-Commercial-ShareAlike (CC BY-NC-SA). This allows faculty to assign these textbooks, and students can read or print copies of chapters or the whole book. However, there are three important limits or conditions: the use must attribute the author and title of the work, it must be for non-commercial purposes, and any derivative uses must be shared-alike and use the same Creative Commons license. The authors retain the copyright of their work, and if requested, the authors are supported in placing their work for sale as an affordable print book in Amazon's CreateSpace, a print-on-demand service.

A print edition is an important offering because some 60 percent of students prefer paying for an affordable print copy of a free open textbook rather than merely having access to the online textbook, according to a survey from the Student Public Interest Research Group.[4] In addition, any royalty from the sale of the print edition goes to the author or to whom they designate, which is an added incentive to publish open textbooks with our program. An important point to clarify is that the online version remains free to everyone from the Open SUNY Textbook catalog.

This ambitious and innovative program published the first five of fifteen open textbooks one year after approving the manuscript proposals. The other ten titles are in various stages of publication, scheduled for 2014. The Open SUNY Textbook program also received a renewal IITG funding for $60,000 to start another call for authors and expand the program with another fifteen titles by the end of 2015. The second pilot also added more participating SUNY libraries, and there is interest outside SUNY to run a parallel program hosted by our Open Monograph Press (OMP), the open-source publishing platform we utilize for our publishing catalog. OMP was recently released by the Public Knowledge Project (http://pkp.sfu.ca) and provides a streamlined, web-based author-submission-workflow and catalog of books.

The team will be applying what they learned from the first pilot, aiming to build a sustainable open textbook program that scales. Potential growth for this program could include 64 SUNY campuses, City University of New York, and other New York libraries, ideally growing into a statewide or regional library publishing initiative. In addition, the next pilot will include an enhanced selection process that encourages participating libraries to consult with their local faculty using a blind proposal review that ranks the likely adoption of proposed manuscripts. This selection-review process evaluates the manuscript proposal's strengths and weaknesses and market conditions, and seeks the best peer reviewers. This collaborative strategy encourages discussions between faculty members and librarians about courses and course resources, and it will enhance the awareness of the cost of textbooks, alternatives such as open textbooks, and the Open SUNY Textbook program.

Developing Local for Global Scale

To develop a cooperative open textbook publishing program, we had to build our capacity for an academic-friendly publishing service. For SUNY Geneseo's Milne Library, that was done for library publishing services with several key hires, role assignment, and projects. First among our hires was Joe Easterly, our Electronic Resources and Digital Scholarship librarian, who helped infuse digital scholarship roles in Technical Services through a text encoding project called Digital Thoreau (http://digitalthoreau.org). Kate Pitcher, head of Technical Services, and her dedicated staff added publishing services to the role of the department. Technical Services staff are an ideal choice given their expertise in metadata and detailed projects. Another key hire to support and enhance the publishing platforms was Leah Root, our Publishing Web Services developer. We also hired Allison Brown as our editor and production manager, an indispensable role for our publishing services. These were all crucial investments to allocate necessary staffing, resources, expertise, and support to growing our publishing capacity.

We also established an eight-member publishing team to focus discussions and develop infrastructure and platforms that the library would support, such as Open Monograph Press for monographs, Open Journal Systems for journals, Omeka for digital collections, and WordPress for communities.

In 2012, Milne Library started publishing reprints of special collection works in the public domain. The first five projects gave us the opportunity to develop and refine publishing workflows. By May of 2013 we published our first new work, *Tagging Along*, by Stuart Symington Jr., a memoir that incorporated several images from our special collections. Many thanks to support from Liz Argentieri, our Special Collections librarian, and to Sheryl Rhodes, our Instruction librarian, for her copyediting services.

Publishing the *Library Publishing Toolkit* in August 2013 (www.publishing toolkit.org) was an invaluable project that helped build our understanding of best practices and strategies for library publishing. The eight-month collaboration between SUNY Geneseo and the Monroe County Library System, with Allison Brown serving as editor, managed the call for authors and resulting compilation of 36 articles about the development of publishing services by public and academic libraries. This project served as an applied research project that helped us gather much needed case studies and strategies and build our expertise with editorial and publishing workflows.

Developing the Open SUNY Textbook program is our most ambitious and innovative publishing program. The rapid prototyping and the variety of collaborations make this publishing initiative uniquely adapted to producing high-quality open textbooks and helping define academic-friendly publishing. Together with talent from across the SUNY libraries and faculty, we have already made an impact. One week after publishing two open textbooks during Open-access Week on October 23, 2013, our Open SUNY Textbook catalog had 1,349 new visitors, 20 percent of them from abroad.

Looking forward, the program's iteration will include refinements to improve efficiency and effectiveness, and it will increase the number of participants. Important factors to assess: what worked well, what we can improve, how to grow the collaboration, how to market for adoption and authoring, and most importantly, the impact on student learning. We are interested in working with others who are developing similar programs. Our vision is to develop a robust infrastructure to support the evolution of open textbook publishing. This includes modular personalization by faculty as well as learning analytics combined with a friendly suite of tools to create, manage, and share interactive learning objects in flexible learning environments. These are critical features to address the rapidly evolving nature and needs of higher education.

The need to support faculty in the production of open textbooks is clearly becoming more evident:

> "Publishers do, however, hoard enormous war chests from sales of educational materials, and we should question whether they have taken control of teaching and learning processes that would be more appropriately owned and overseen by academics . . .

> "Ultimately, I chose . . . publishing open textbooks . . . because it gave me the greatest control over my project and the potential for the greatest impact . . .

> We need to realize our power as authors and publishers. Working collaboratively, we can create dynamic teaching and learning environments."[5]

Libraries are increasingly aware that in collaboration with faculty, they can help solve one of the critical issues facing higher education: the rising cost of a college education. By focusing on open textbooks and open educational resource publishing, we strengthen the position of our faculty and colleges at a time of rapid changes in higher education. Libraries have experienced and successfully navigated the rapidly evolving learning environment early and have changed significantly. In order to connect faculty author to reader and teacher to learner in sustainable ways, librarians are tapping into their connector and curation expertise to provide faculty authors. Together libraries can lower the cost of education by developing important and useful networks between authors, readers, teachers, and learners. The Open SUNY Textbook program launched thanks to SUNY's IITG grant funding, and its progression is due to the collaborations of all the librarians and libraries involved in the planning and operations of the program—especially to the faculty authors and peer reviewers.

Notes

1. "2012 Florida Student Textbook Survey," 2012, www.openaccesstextbooks.org/pdf/2012_Florida_Student_Textbook_Survey.pdf.
2. U.S. Government Accountability Office, "College Textbooks: Students Have Greater Access to Textbook Information: Report to Congressional Committees," 2013, www.gao.gov/products/GAO-13-368.
3. The State University of New York, "Provost Announcement 2012 Innovative Instruction Technology Grants," 2012, accessed March 1, 2014, www.suny.edu/provost/IITGProvostAnnouncement.cfm.
4. Student Public Interest Research Group, "New Report Finds Switching to Open Textbooks Saves Students Thousands" (September 30, 2010, www.studentpirgs.org/news/new-report-finds-switching-open-textbooks-saves-students-thousands.
5. Joe Moxley, "Open Textbook Publishing: Who Is Best Suited to Control Textbooks: The Faculty or the Publishers?" *Academe* (September/October 2013), www.aaup.org/article/open-textbook-publishing#.UqOtYWbnbL8.

Interstate Library Delivery

Kathleen Drozd

Need

- to build strong cross-state delivery connections
- to keep the cost of delivery low for all involved
- to improve turnaround time for resource sharing and delivery for participating libraries and partnering states

Benefit

- strengthening ties with libraries in our neighboring state
- saving resources, such as staff time and packaging materials
- providing patrons with access to collections of multiple states quickly and at a reasonable price

Minitex is a three-state library network that serves Minnesota, North Dakota, and South Dakota. It has a strong resource-sharing program in all three states that is supported by a delivery network comprised of commercial couriers who deliver book loans, audiovisual material, photocopies, and other resources requested by library patrons. Material is delivered overnight five days a week to most libraries in the Minitex region. Other smaller libraries that are not on the Minitex courier route receive service through the United Parcel Service (UPS).

Minitex delivery staff sort and pack close to 1 million items each year. The five full-time employees work from 7 a.m.–11 p.m. six days a week to sort and pack deliveries that come in from the multiple couriers throughout the day. The goal is to move all materials out of the office by the end of each working day.

OCLC codes are used for routing materials into the correct tubs, and OCLC-like codes have been created for libraries not on that service. The tubs are secured with white plastic zip ties, and clippers are provided to all of the libraries for cutting the zip ties. The ties have helped keep theft and damage rates low. No packing material is used but there has been very little damage to materials in transit. The tubs are delivered and picked up at a secured loading dock at various times through the day. The tubs are then placed on a conveyor that transports them 82 feet up to the sorting area.

We developed a light-hearted website called "Del the Book" to inform staff of the more than 800 libraries to which the courier service either delivers to or connects to. Del has been a big hit with many of our participating libraries; it can be viewed at http://minitex.umn.edu/Delivery/Tour.

Minitex has always considered local resource sharing and delivery to be the best way to serve library patrons. To support that goal, it provides last mile grants to major library locations that act as part of the larger hub-and-spoke delivery system. Delivery is via commercial courier to either a major academic library or at a regional public library system in the state. These libraries are responsible for moving the material to libraries in their region. Some of these regional library systems are very large and move several million items annually, with Minitex materials joining the library's internal delivery system. For example, the courier drops multiple tubs at Minnesota State University–Moorhead; the interlibrary loan staff at the library pull their materials out and add their materials into tubs that are going to other libraries in their area, such as Concordia College, North Dakota State University, Lake Agassiz Regional Library, and Fargo Public Library.

Minitex has contracts with both North Dakota and South Dakota to provide a slightly different delivery service. In North Dakota it contracts with a courier company for only a few stops in several major cities. The materials are sent via the courier directly to the larger library locations and returned in the same manner. UPS is used for the low-volume library locations. In South Dakota Minitex contracts with the courier company that runs the South Dakota Courier Delivery Service. The materials from Minnesota and

South Dakota libraries all come into Sioux Falls, are sorted, and then reach the rest of the state through a second hub-and-spoke delivery system.

While we have always considered the three states (Minnesota, North Dakota, and South Dakota) as our primary region, Minitex also connects its delivery service to Wisconsin, where we maintain a long-standing reciprocal borrowing program. From 1983 to 2001, Minitex's delivery service dropped into Wisconsin at the University of Wisconsin, Madison. The University of Wisconsin library staff pulled out their items from the tubs and sorted the remaining materials to go on to the South Central Library Services (SCLS) regional delivery services for distribution to other Wisconsin libraries. The same process was used by Wisconsin libraries to send materials to Minitex.

In 2001, Minitex staff traveled to Madison, Wisconsin, to meet with the state library staff to discuss improving delivery services. The group decided to change the Wisconsin drop-off stop to the headquarters office of SCLS and to have their staff sort and distribute to all Wisconsin libraries. Through the University of Minnesota, Minitex is part of the Committee on Institutional Cooperation's (CIC) reciprocal borrowing program, and so materials bound for the University of Wisconsin, Madison, travel directly via separate courier contract.

In the discussion in 2001, we learned that SCLS was contracting with a delivery company (Waltco, Inc.) to provide delivery to five northern Wisconsin counties. We work with Waltco to have their drivers pick up materials, which were presorted and packed in specifically labeled tubs, for those five northern counties at the Minitex office. These materials were then piggy-backed on the SCLS materials going to those county libraries. These libraries were now receiving overnight delivery and pickup to the Minitex office.

Once the Wisconsin delivery routes were set, we decided to split the cost evenly and not be concerned about the volume of material being shipped. All items moved through physical delivery are returnable items, which means each item makes two trips. We worked with the frontline staff to determine the types of labeling and routing slips that would be needed. Minitex's general practice is to use the OCLC code, while SCLS uses a more descriptive code. We decided to use the current label structure at each headquarters office to see how delivery staff felt about using two different coding systems. After a short time, sorting staff in both operations became comfortable using the two types of codes. In 2011–2012, approximately 50,000 items moved on this route. Wisconsin State Library and Minitex each pay approximately $450 a year for the interstate shipment.

Our primary region of Minnesota, North Dakota, and South Dakota has a long history of contracts that set high library staff expectations on resource sharing and delivery. The work we did on improved delivery in Wisconsin was accomplished more through a partnership and discussion of how to improve services, and both states are pleased with the improvements. Our interconnected, long-standing delivery service has provided low-cost delivery service in support of resource sharing to four states, with great benefit to the patrons of the region.

Open-Source Integrated Library Systems: A Consortial Implementation of Evergreen

Randy Dykhuis

Need

- Michigan has a statewide resource-sharing system, MeLCat, that is able to accommodate a variety of local integrated library systems (ILS), but some libraries have PC-based or outdated systems that make participation in MeLCat difficult.
- Many of these libraries are small and unable to afford the costs to migrate to a full-featured commercial ILS, which would enhance their ability to use MeLCat.
- The Library of Michigan (LM) created MeLCat in 2004 and contracts with the Midwest Collaborative for Library Services (MCLS) to operate the system.

Benefit

- With a newer ILS, small libraries could offer better service to their patrons and strengthen their access to MeLCat.
- Open-source software made it possible to offer a full-featured ILS at a lower price than comparable commercial systems.
- Offering Evergreen was a way for MCLS to offer more value to

member libraries, and it was a natural extension of the organization's work with LM to support and implement MeLCat.

- Awareness of Evergreen was high and many libraries indicated a strong interest in considering migration to the system, including one of the largest public libraries in Michigan, the Grand Rapids Public Library (GRPL).

In 2008, MCLS and GRPL became partners to lead the development of Michigan Evergreen, a shared open-source integrated library system, which was open to any Michigan library.[1] After announcing its formation, MCLS quickly found a core of seven libraries interested in joining the group, and the first library, Branch District Library, completed its migration to Evergreen and went live in August 2008. The others soon followed. A detailed report about Michigan Evergreen's start can be found in *Collaborative Librarianship* (www.collaborativelibrarianship.org).[2]

After a strong start, the number of libraries joining Michigan Evergreen soon stalled at 11, and by the end of 2011, it was evident that MCLS would not be able to sustain Michigan Evergreen. MCLS was spending much more on support, training, and infrastructure than it was generating in revenue from the participating libraries. The participating libraries paid a fee that was based on the size of their collection and the number of patron records, plus a small flat fee that was paid regardless of size. With only 11 participating libraries, there was not enough revenue coming in to cover all the costs.

There were no indications that the number of participants in Michigan Evergreen would increase. In addition to the slow growth of the group, some participants were interested in other options. One decided to migrate to OCLC's WorldShare Management Services and another to contract with a different Evergreen hosting agency.

When it became apparent that MCLS would not be able to continue supporting the group, MCLS initiated a discussion with the group's library directors about Michigan Evergreen's future. After openly discussing the issues with the directors and examining and discarding several possibilities, MCLS took the difficult step of announcing that it would cease support for the group by June 30, 2015. The directors had several options at that point:

1. They could each go on their own to another hosting agency of their choice.
2. They could stay with MCLS for the next year or two while researching their options and then make individual decisions.
3. They could remain together as a group and find a hosting agency that would support Michigan Evergreen as a shared system.

In the end, the majority decided on the last option. GRPL decided to remain on Evergreen but run it themselves on a locally hosted server.

MCLS brokered quotes for the remaining libraries, and two hosting agencies—Equinox Software and LYRASIS—submitted proposals. After further research and discussion with the directors, six libraries voted to move to LYRASIS as soon as possible. MCLS, GRPL, and LYRASIS worked together to ensure a problem-free and timely migration. By June 30, 2012, all six libraries were up and running on servers housed and managed at LYRASIS, and MCLS ceased involvement with the daily operations of Michigan Evergreen.

How did Michigan Evergreen go from growth and bright promise in 2008 to stasis followed by dissolution in 2012? It is a cautionary tale that may hold lessons for other consortia to consider before tackling an open-source project like Evergreen.

First and most importantly, the source of funding matters a great deal. When MCLS and GRPL began discussing a joint project to build a shared system, there was much more enthusiasm about Evergreen than experience with the software. Many libraries in Michigan were saying that they thought open-source software offered great promise and they would be very interested in migrating to a system like Evergreen.

With the formation of Michigan Evergreen, MCLS devised a cost-sharing formula that was based on size of collection and number of patron records, plus a small flat annual fee. Every library was responsible for paying its own way. There was no outside funding to support the project through its initial few years. The lack of external financial support was a critical error.

Georgia, Indiana, Massachusetts, and South Carolina all have large shared Evergreen systems. Each of them uses federal and/or state funding to cover some or all of the costs for participation in Evergreen. Clearly these subsidies make it much more attractive to libraries and much easier to migrate to the shared system. Without funding of this sort, MCLS had to rely on libraries to pay the full cost of operating the system, and for many small libraries, that put Michigan Evergreen out of their reach. Large libraries could afford to compare to commercial companies such as SirsiDynix, Polaris, and Innovative Interfaces, and often the commercial systems had features that were still in development in Evergreen.

The financial model for Michigan Evergreen mandated that the group contain a mixture of large and small libraries, which did not happen. Although there was serious interest from a few large public libraries, none came on board with Michigan Evergreen. There were several reasons for this: (1) the library's current vendor sometimes offered very attractive financial terms for the library to stay with them, (2) Evergreen lacked functionality that some libraries deemed necessary, or (3) the library was uncomfortable with open-source software. Without participation from some large libraries, Michigan Evergreen could not generate the revenue needed to sustain itself.

Second, based on its funding model, there were not enough potential member libraries in Michigan to reach the scale needed to survive. To be successful, MCLS needed between 50 and 75 libraries, and there were not enough candidates among Michigan libraries to reach a sustainable level. To reach that scale would have required a commitment to marketing and sales in other regions. However, these are activities that are ancillary to MCLS's core mission of service to its member libraries. With start-up funding from an outside source, perhaps MCLS could have mounted the kind of sustained sales and marketing effort necessary to generate the scale required for Michigan Evergreen to succeed. Absent that funding source, MCLS could not undertake that kind of effort.

Third, the Michigan Evergreen group was ad hoc without a natural constituency. The existing shared systems in Michigan are mostly run by public library cooperatives and are organized along geographic boundaries. The libraries in these systems know each other and, over the years, have worked together on other projects. These established relationships make it easier to solve the inevitable problems and challenges that arise on complex projects like this. In Michigan Evergreen there was no shared history to rely on. Everything was new, and small issues occasionally escalated unnecessarily. In addition, MCLS and GRPL had never tackled a large collaborative project and had to develop polices, processes, and procedures for Michigan

Evergreen without the benefits that a history of successful collaboration brings.

Fourth, MCLS was often seen as the vendor, and participating libraries came to the group with the same expectations that they would have had of a commercial vendor. The libraries that considered Evergreen did not view it as joining a collaborative effort of peers but rather as akin to buying an ILS from a vendor. MCLS was never able to transcend this view and make Michigan Evergreen a member-owned cooperative.

In summary, MCLS misread the marketplace and misjudged the number of libraries that were ready to commit to an open-source ILS. In addition, the financial model required a larger geographic area than MCLS was prepared to cultivate with marketing and sales efforts. Finally, the software was not mature enough and lacked significant features that would attract large public libraries. All of these reasons contributed to MCLS's inability to create a sustainable user base for Michigan Evergreen.

Notes

1. In 2010, the Michigan Library Consortium merged with the Indiana Cooperative Library Services Authority to form the Midwest Collaborative for Library Services (MCLS). MCLS continued to offer many of the services from the two legacy organizations, including Michigan Evergreen.
2. Randy Dykhuis, "Michigan Evergreen: Implementing a Shared Open Source Integrated Library System," *Collaborative Librarianship* 1, no. 2 (2009): 60–65.

Open-Source Software and Consortium Governance Structure

Vicki Teal Lovely

Need

- a shared integrated library system
- a robust collaboration with an impetus to make software development a hands-on activity
- a cloud-based vendor solution that offers training, support, and more

Benefit

- software development to meet specific needs of participating libraries
- a system shaped to meet the specific needs of a large public library system

The South Central Library System (SCLS) has offered a shared integrated library system (ILS) to its public library members since the mid-1980s. Since SCLS' inception, the consortium has had a strong governance structure in place, with each library voting on issues based on a divided membership formula. Costs were also shared, based on a similar formula, and included ILS software fees, cataloging, and third-party products. Library directors met regularly as the Library Interchange NetworK (LINK) consortium to make policy and directional decisions regarding the shared ILS (LINKcat). LINK has both a strong history of member participation and a strong peer relationship regarding enforcement of policies. In 2008, following an extensive investigation of existing integrated library system software by a selection committee and with input from all consortium members, LINK chose to go with a Koha-based, open-source ILS. LibLime was selected as a support vendor for the following reasons:

- Existing propriety ILS software at the time did not offer substantial improvements over the old but robust Dynix system.
- Open-source software offered a risk management strategy in that the libraries could drive software development that would be specific to their needs.
- The Koha ILS was more developed at the time than the other major open-source ILS software, Evergreen.
- Choosing a vendor such as LibLime would provide the training, support, data migration, and software development without the need to increase infrastructure.
- LibLime was the most established Koha support vendor in the United States.

The possibility of driving software development was particularly appealing to the consortium members. SCLS staff had spent a substantial amount of time working with a prospective vendor to ensure that the next generation ILS would meet the complex needs of a large public library consortium. Once Koha was selected, the ability to develop the software became a shared goal, and much collaboration centered on this goal.

Selecting an open-source ILS is often seen as a means to reduce costs. The LINK consortium did expect to save money on software licenses but did not expect to save money overall, as the funds that would have been saved were targeted toward improving the software. A scoping study of Koha had been conducted as part of the evaluation process and identified a significant number of needed improvements. Since the libraries had a shared goal of shaping the software to meet library needs, they determined that ongoing development of the software would be budgeted. In an open-source model, software development done by one library is shared by all other libraries using the system. Software development committees consisting of library staff were established. These committees prioritized development projects and then worked with LibLime to develop specifications. Another role of committee members was to help with testing the software.

A consortium that chooses open-source software will need to decide whether or not to participate in system development, and funds should be budgeted accordingly. An open-source ILS such as Koha can be implemented as a turnkey solution, but SCLS and the LINK libraries had the budget and the impetus to make software development a hands-on activity.

Another important decision that the consortium faced was whether to host the software locally or to take advantage of the hosting services offered by the vendor. The committee formed to investigate hosting options decided that a vendor-based, cloud-hosted solution would save resources, as the vendor would provide all routine maintenance and backups that we would need to do if hosted locally. The cloud-hosted option also provided disaster recovery, redundant backups, and more rapid expansion of server space. Since the LINK consortium made this decision, cloud-hosting has become common even with propriety ILSs.

The Koha implementation was originally slated for 2010. At this time, SCLS was implementing a change in governance structure. This change was due to a variety of factors, but in part it was to address the concern that the LINK consortium had a very large governing body. Decision-making was perceived as cumbersome by the 41 participating public libraries. With input from libraries, SCLS decided to go to a representative form of governance. Libraries were divided into clusters, and each cluster elected a representative to serve on the various committees, including the ILS Committee and the Administrative Council. Members voted to end the LINK consortium. All library committees now are advisory to SCLS, and SCLS offers the ILS as a service to its members.

SCLS left in place the development committees that focused on Koha migration issues and software development, and the module committees that set shared policies for the libraries and determined standardized settings and options. These working groups allowed SCLS libraries to continue to have a substantial amount of involvement in the direction that SCLS takes Koha.

A variety of circumstances caused a delay in the implementation of Koha until April 2011. The data migration process went extremely well. However, modifications made to the software were being beta tested at the same time libraries were implementing the new software. Migrating to any new system is stressful, but facing unexpected bugs was not something that had been anticipated. On top of this, there were response-time problems. The most serious response-time problems were resolved relatively quickly by the vendor, but it took longer to fix bugs.

Because of the change in governance structure, the process for escalation of grievances was no longer clear. Libraries were now meeting in smaller groups (clusters) and lost the benefit of the larger LINK consortium; they no longer were able to share problems and experiences with all of the libraries participating in the system. Cluster representatives were expected to disseminate information to their member libraries on private cluster lists on which SCLS did not participate. Information was not communicated uniformly, and sometimes it was not delivered at all. Different clusters reacted differently to the problems with Koha, and it was not always clear what the priorities were for resolving the problems. Ultimately, we developed systems to prioritize the problems, but it was a struggle.

As intended when the governance structure was changed, SCLS is reviewing the new structure with input from the libraries. The chain of communication between SCLS, cluster representatives, and libraries will need to be improved. Cluster boundaries may be realigned to allow better opportunities for meeting. SCLS will respond by focusing on customer service and quality assurance, much as a business would do.

But the need for collaboration with the libraries is as strong as ever. SCLS employees are working closely with existing ILS committees to steer Koha development. We are operating the system for the libraries, and we solicit their input about how best to do so.

As active software developers, we cannot avoid the beta testing process. If we pay for a new feature, we will need to be the first to test it live. We have now established a much more rigorous testing process. We test new features on a sandbox, or backup version of the software, to identify and fix as many bugs as possible. We learned that we need to test all software functionality prior to each new release, not just the areas where development occurred. We ask for library staff volunteers to run through software checklists. This checklists assure that fewer unexpected bugs will crop up once we go live on a new release. As with any software upgrade, there will be new bugs, but we have seen substantial reduction of bugs introduced on the go-live date since we started the more rigorous testing process.

Was open-source the right decision? This question is almost impossible to answer. Due to the problems we experienced with development bugs, open-source has definitely not been an easy solution. Development is hard work and there are almost always bugs in the software. However, bugs are not unique to open-source, as propriety ILS software contain bugs too. With our system, however, the libraries can prioritize which bugs will be fixed first, and they do get fixed. If we have funding, we can choose which development projects we would like to work on. We have recently started to collaborate with other LibLime Koha customers to share development costs, documentation, and experiences. For other libraries considering open-source, it may be worth noting that development is not required, and in fact, very few libraries or consortia using LibLime Koha actually participate in development. The experience of libraries that do not do development will be different as they will not be beta testing.

We recently conducted an evaluation of LibLime Koha to determine whether we should stay with Koha and continue to develop the software or whether we should seek other options. A clear majority of participating libraries said we should continue with Koha. For the foreseeable future, the SCLS shared ILS will continue to evaluate our LibLime Koha implementation annually to see if it is still the right solution.

CASE STUDY 10

Vendor-Based Shared Integrated Library Systems

Jeanine F. Gatzke and Belinda E. Lawrence

Need

- improve service via a consortium that shares an integrated library system (ILS)
- contract with a commercial ILS vendor
- provide twice-daily weekday materials delivery

Benefit

- seamless materials borrowing among the 14 libraries for faculty, staff, and students
- substantial cost savings for eight institutions sharing a single systems administrator
- broad and varied expertise of over 200 talented staff
- cross-institution communication, problem solving, and planning and implementation enhancements facilitated by committees and communities-of-interest

Cooperating Libraries in Consortium (CLIC) is a nonprofit corporation of eight member institutions in the Minneapolis-St. Paul area, including Augsburg College, Bethel University and Seminary, Concordia University, Hamline University and Law School, Macalester College, St Catherine University, University of Northwestern–St. Paul, and the University of St. Thomas Seminary and Law Schools. CLIC was founded in 1969 to support cooperative collection development, interlibrary loan, and document delivery among its member libraries. Since 1987, CLIC's major focus has been a shared Integrated Library System (ILS). In 2001, CLIC migrated from a shared Dynix system to the self-hosted Innovative Interfaces, Inc. (III) Millennium system, and in 2011 the hosting of the system was moved to a server at III. With just under two million bibliographic and over 3.5 million item records in the system, CLIC is the third largest academic system in the state of Minnesota.

CLIC serves fourteen member libraries with over 200 support staff. Our main objective is to "provide improved and more comprehensive library resources and services to library users through the enhanced sharing of materials; to operate and manage an integrated, automated library system; to develop entrepreneurial initiatives in order to deliver new/expanding content and services; and to provide opportunities for staff collegiality, leadership and training."[1]

The CLIC staff consists of three people: an executive director, a system administrator, and an office manager. All direct interaction with the ILS vendor is coordinated through the office staff, primarily via the system administrator. Among his responsibilities are the duties of coordinating any software updates; monitoring system functionality, including issues that are reported to the help desk by individual library staff; running and distributing global reports; representing CLIC to III; and maintaining mailing lists and web services. The member libraries benefit both in cost savings and from the expertise of a central system administrator.

Each ILS module has a few special interest groups and a corresponding operational committee (OC) that meets on a regular basis at the CLIC office to discuss and solve problems, address issues relevant to the academic library world, and to plan and implement enhancements to the shared system. These committees are comprised of appointed representatives from each institution, but their meetings are open to any staff interested in attending. The nine existing OCs are: Acquisitions, Associate System

Administrators, Cataloging, Circulation, Digitization, Interlibrary Loan, OPAC, Reserves, and Serials. Each module-specific OC sends one member representative to the Systems Operations Committee, whose primary goal is to aid in system upgrades and perform specific module testing after any upgrade to verify that the system is operating as expected. The Systems Operations members also share in the responsibility of monitoring the III problem log and updating their OC colleagues on issues and resolutions.

Additionally, CLIC leadership has encouraged the formation of Communities of Interest (COI) and task forces to address specific issues. The COIs tend to be more long-lasting in nature and have a narrow focus, while the task forces form and disband on an ad hoc basis. There are currently nine COIs meeting regularly: A/V, Authority Control, Batch Loading, Collection Development, Electronic Resources, Reference, Student Employees, Web, and WorldCat Local. Task forces most often arise out of OC or COI meetings to focus on a short-term commitment and then disband once the task is complete. An added benefit of the various meeting types is the development of personal relationships across institutional lines, which become valuable resources when issues arise and input from another site is sought. All operational committees and COIs have a designated liaison from the consortium office to ensure consistent and accurate communication between/among groups and within the consortium as a whole.

One of the primary benefits of a shared ILS that is most appreciated by CLIC patrons is their ability to borrow an item from another CLIC institution. With the click of the request button, the desired book is pulled from the shelf by the owning library, submitted to the courier, and delivered to the user's designated pickup location. To support this delivery function, an independent delivery contractor makes deliveries of materials between member institutions on a twice-daily basis throughout the regular school year. His route also includes two additional local seminary libraries and the University of Minnesota/Minitex, which allows CLIC resources to be shared statewide through the state's resource-sharing network (MnLINK). For the past ten years, the contractor has guaranteed delivery of materials requested between CLIC member institutions in half a day to two days.

Over time the consortium has evolved from its original intent of sharing an ILS and document delivery into an organization that also shares people resources and knowledge, including teaching, training, and troubleshooting. It also fosters innovation. For example, two institutions in the consortia had earlier adopted new interlibrary loan software. Over the years, as the success of the product was made known, it became clear to the other members that this software also should be adopted by their institutions. With the help of the first two adopters, the other libraries followed suit. Learning from the early-adopter libraries saved money that would have been spent on professional trainers or travel time. In addition, fellow CLIC colleagues were on hand when needed throughout the adoption process and will be available in the future. Procedures also needed to be tweaked consortium-wide and successfully integrated into the workflow of each institution.

There are a prolific number of examples of cooperation among libraries and staff. They are varied and occur in both the public and technical service realms and in areas concerned both with the ILS and outside of it. For a number of years the Authority Control COI has sponsored a day-long workshop in January for catalogers and other staff working with authority control to discuss a specific topic related to their work within our ILS or in response to changes in national standards. Occasionally a guest speaker is brought in, but more often the discussion is led by members of the COI who have delved deeply into a topic and are willing to share their expertise. The workshop always includes time to work on authority headings as a group and to crowd-source answers to questions that arise.

Sharing an ILS has fostered an atmosphere of collegiality that makes it natural to consider how any decision made will affect the other institutions prior to its implementation. Cooperation among member libraries and staff has been the key to an enhanced service experience for users from all member institutions. It is the commitment of library staff and CLIC staff that makes the consortium work.

CLIC has recently begun the search for a next generation system to replace the current ILS. In the decade since we purchased the current ILS, there has been a substantial change in the nature of our individual library collections. We have gone from print-based to electronic resources, and our libraries must subscribe to additional services to manage those resources. The lack of fit with our current ILS has created concerns and issues of relevancy and efficiency for the continued use of the current system, as well as the recognition that often we are no longer meeting our users, at their point of need, with all resources discoverable and accessible from a single source.

As CLIC libraries explore the systems that are available, they are looking for specific features that will allow them to meet future as well as current needs. The libraries want a system that is responsive and scalable, highly fault-tolerant, flexible and extensible, and centrally hosted as well as one that integrates with other systems.

Moving the old system into the cloud is not an acceptable option. CLIC is looking for a system that will take advantage of new architecture designed to handle our current and future collections. The consortium wants the new system to streamline workflows by reducing task duplication and increasing automated tasks, and desires a robust assessment and reporting component along with the continued ability to efficiently share resources.

As part of the search process, CLIC is also looking at its own future. For the past 26 years the consortium's focus has been the ILS; however, this relationship is dynamic and changing. Where is it heading? What role could and should the consortium play for its members? With a stable working relationship and the shared ILS acting as the nucleus, CLIC has gone beyond the central tenet to share people, resources, and other software. All indications are that our commitment to sharing will continue long into the future.

Note

1. Karen Harwood, "Cooperating Libraries in Consortium History," December 1, 2010.
2. http://clic.edu/newclic/dir/structure/COOPERATING%20LIBRARIES%20IN% 20CONSORTIUM%20HISTORY.pdf.

Enhancing Access to History: Collaborative Digital Initiatives

Liz Bishoff

Need

- scholars must travel long distances to reach libraries' special collections and archives
- national education standards require students to utilize primary source materials as part of their educational programs
- many special collections and archives have restricted-use policies that make accessing the collections difficult

Benefit

- expands access and the ability to interact with special collections and archives
- creates many new users for rare and unique materials
- enhances educational use of primary source materials across all age groups
- unites collections spread across more than one institution through digitization of the items

Generations of students, scholars, and researchers have had to identify and then travel to sometimes distant libraries and archives in order to access special collections and unique resources. Time, distance, and policy restrictions limited who could use the collections. As early as the mid-1980s, national libraries and major museums began exploring strategies for expanding access to their collections by making them available on the nascent Internet. Within a decade major research libraries had established projects to digitize heavily used and unique collections. Digitization of collections offered libraries and cultural heritage organizations a means of overcoming barriers to access.

One of the key outcomes of these early initiatives was the virtual reunification of distributed collections. Museums holding the artifacts developed projects with libraries and archives that held print and photograph collections. At the same time, novel uses for new audiences of these collections were developed, with a particular emphasis on support of K–20 education needs and local history researchers. By the mid–2000s, more than 30 states had developed statewide or regional collaborative digital initiatives, encouraged in part by the Institute for Museum and Library Services (IMLS) National Leadership Grant program, and Library Services and Technology Act (LSTA) grant initiatives from state libraries.

Collaborative digital initiatives have developed at the national, state, regional, and local level. Sometimes the collaboration is across library types, while more frequently it brings together libraries and other cultural heritage institutions (e.g., museums, archives, historical societies). On a national level these collaborative efforts are subject focused, such as the Bio-Diversity Heritage Library (www.biodiversitylibrary.org). More recently we are seeing the development of national/international digital libraries, such as Europeana, a collaborative effort across the European Union countries (www.europeana.eu); The World Digital Library, an initiative led by UNESCO/Library of Congress; and the developing Digital Public Library of America (DPLA) (http://dp.la).

At the local level we see the development of digital partnerships to capture local heritage, with the local public or academic library partnering with the local historical society. Many of these partnerships are supported by a regional, multitype library consortium. Several examples include:

- Southeastern New York Regional Library Council's (SENYLRC) Hudson River Valley Heritage (www.hrvh.org/index.htm), a collaborative established in 2001 to provide access to historic resources of the Hudson River Valley

- New York Heritage Digital Collections (www.newyorkheritage .org/), a shared site for the nine New York regional libraries, which until 2013 had operated their own sites. It incorporates content from *Tools of History*, *CNY Heritage*, *WNY Legacy*, *CDLC Digital Collections*, *Long Island Memories*, *North Country Digital History*, *Digital Metro*, *Finger Lakes and Genesee River Valley (FLAG) Heritage*, and *Hudson River Valley Heritage*. Several of these regional councils, including SENYLRC, have continued to operate their own platform.

Barriers to participation in these collaborative efforts included lack of technical infrastructure to create and provide access to digital collections, lack of knowledge and expertise with the new digital standards and best practices, lack of funding to create digital collections, and lack of knowledge about long-term maintenance of digital collections. At the same time, new technologies, such as social media, offered new opportunities for building awareness of digital collections. With social media cultural heritage organizations have been able to engage their local communities. The Maine Memory Network has developed programs that have their partners engage with K–12 schools and community groups in identifying locally held collections, scanning and creating metadata for these collections, and then adding the collections to the Network. Teachers and students can then use those collections, along with other resources, in the Maine Memory Network in their studies.

Digital collaboration offers a range of leadership opportunities for library consortia. Over the past decade library consortia have provided the vision of how digital collections can advance the mission of their members. Common responses of library consortia to the development of collaborative digital collections include supporting technological infrastructure with digital asset management systems, server space, and back-up strategies. Additionally the consortia provide support and training as well as access to grant funding to support creation of digital collections. These collaborative efforts result in the creation of high-quality digital content based on common digital standards and best practices, increased discoverability, and most important, expanded access to the collections across a region.

There are a variety of collaborative digital models. Among the most successful are those that are managed by statewide agencies, such as state historical societies or state libraries. The successful programs have common elements, including programmatic leadership and advocacy, a multicultural heritage network, quality collections based on standards and best practices, support and training, funding that ensures stability, and community engagement.

The Minnesota Digital Library (MDL) incorporates many of the elements for success. A collaboration of more than 160 libraries and cultural heritage organizations, the MDL is funded by the Minnesota Arts and Cultural Heritage Fund of the Minnesota Clean Water, Land, and Legacy Constitutional Amendment. It is administered by Minitex. More than 150,000 digital resources are available through MDL's primary database, *Minnesota Reflections*, Management of the project is shared by staff from Minitex, University of Minnesota Libraries, St. Cloud University Libraries, Minnesota History Society, and others.

The creation of digital resources is guided by standards and best practices adopted by MDL participants. Based on Dublin Core Metadata Schema, MDL has expanded the structure to incorporate elements unique to the Minnesota project, including Minnesota Cities and Town's geographic terms. All partners are required to create their own metadata; they have the option of creating their own digital contents or outsourcing it to a third party under contract with Minitex. CONTENTdm is used to manage the digital collections, making them available across Minnesota. In the past year, MDL was selected as one of six hub sites for the Digital Public Library of America, furthering discovery of the MDL collections. "In the first four months, MDL has seen a 23 percent increase in object usage from DPLA referrals," reported Valerie Horton, Minitex's executive director.

As with many collaborative digital programs, MDL's priority is expanded use of digital collections by the K–12 educational community. Historians and educators are part of MDL's Selection Committee, and lesson plans have been created that incorporate the Minnesota Reflections digital collections. Guides to Minnesota Reflections were created by teachers who are familiar with the Minnesota K–12 teaching standards. These guides include tips on how to search Minnesota Reflections and ideas for developing lesson plans from the guides.

The Maine Memory Network (MMN) (www.mainememory.net), recognized as a national model for an online museum, is led by the Maine Historical Society. With more than 275 partners across Maine, the MMN has transformed how the historical society is perceived in the state. It began as an online digital archive with the goal of expanding access to historical collection, and then evolved into a flexible online museum.

Maine Historical Society has created a model that captures the history of the state while building new opportunities for engaging with that history. It has accomplished that with these ingredients: a technological platform designed to meet the needs and skill level of the partner organizations, programmatic activities that incorporate common standards and best practices, incentive funding for new initiatives, support and training for partner organizations, and statewide advocacy targeted to both cultural heritage organizations and the residents of Maine.

In addition to the contributing partner program, MMN has developed programs that encourage engagement with K–12 schools as well as others in the community. The result is a shared creation of the digital record of Maine. Web exhibits created by the MMN and contributing partners present the stories of Maine, pulling content from across the collections. A "My Album" feature allows individuals to create their own stories, once again pulling content from across the collections. As a result, unique views of Maine are emerging.

The role of cultural heritage organizations will continue to expand in the digital world, in part because these organizations hold the record of our communities' history. To expand access to this history, cultural heritage organizations need assistance from those who can enable their participation in the digital world. Library consortia are well positioned to play this enabling role. Consortia have expertise in managing the technical environment required to support digital collections and can support these organizations as they create and provide access to digital collections. The use of social media, the addition of these collections to websites, and the use of e-commerce to order copies are all within the consortia's area of expertise. Consortia are experienced in negotiating contracts for digital conversion services and software licensing. Through their connections with school libraries, consortia can engage the K–12 community with the cultural heritage community. Consortia also have experience in grant writing, so they can help obtain incentive funding to get new organizations involved in digitizing collections and support innovation in the use of digital content.

Shared Physical Depository: The Five College Library Depository

Jay Schafer

Need

- limited shelving capacity
- high costs of building expansions to campus libraries

Benefit

- recouped shelf space on multiple campuses
- anticipated savings of 75 percent in storage costs

The Robert Frost Library at Amherst College in Amherst, Massachusetts, opened in 1965, and by 1989 it was clearly time to plan for additional shelving capacity. Surprised by the estimated $26 to $29 million expansion cost to renovate the Frost Library, the College went looking for less-expensive solutions. Coincidentally in 1992 the Federal Reserve was planning to auction a 44,000-square foot Strategic Air Command Base it had acquired from the U.S. Air Force. The facility, commonly referred to as "the bunker," was built into the side of the Mount Holyoke Range about four miles from Amherst College. After Amherst College acquired the 26-acre site and structure, it soon became apparent that it was very well suited to be an off-site storage facility for library materials, and within several years, 75,000 volumes were transferred from Frost Library to the bunker.[1]

The Five College Libraries (the libraries of Amherst College, Hampshire College, Mount Holyoke College, Smith College, and the University of Massachusetts-Amherst) have a long history of successful collaboration in many areas, including acquisitions, cataloging, circulation, electronic resource management, and materials delivery. Like Frost Library, each of the other libraries was running out of space. The libraries were also meeting resistance from campus administration about the high cost of building expansion. Although there was initial concern about a central book depository in the Five Colleges Librarians Council (FCLC), their history of cooperation, the high level of trust among the five, and the considerable encouragement from their presidents to expand coordination of collection development and collection maintenance convinced the FCLC to move forward with a shared physical book depository.

In 1998, the Five College's Board of Directors authorized the creation of a Five College Library Depository (FCLD). FCLC then approached the Andrew W. Mellon Foundation to fund a planning grant to explore the rental of 10,000 square feet of space in the Amherst College bunker to create the Five College Libraries Depository as a place for storing one copy of little-used print journals and books. Duplicate copies could then be de-accessed by other libraries, saving space in the on-campus libraries that held copies of each little-used item. The FCLD was to function as a shared collection from which any of the Five College libraries could recall a print copy or a facsimile of an article. Storage cost in the FCLD was estimated to be less than one-fourth the cost of storage on campus. With a total capacity estimated at 500,000 volumes, it was estimated that the University of Massachusetts would provide about 55 percent of the contributions, while Amherst and Smith would each provide about 16 percent, Mount Holyoke 12 percent, and Hampshire 1 percent.[2]

All campuses would be beneficiaries of the shared collection and the Last Copy Policy by creating space in their on-campus shelving regardless of which campus contributed materials directly to the FCLD. Of note, the Last Copy Policy states that a library may not de-accession the last copy of a work held in the Five College libraries unless that last copy is in the FCLD. Contributions from the private colleges would become property of the consortium; contributions from the University would remain property of the University but would be committed to shared use.

In 2000, the Amherst College Board of Trustees authorized the leasing of 10,000 square feet to be used as the Five College Library Depository. Five Colleges raised $1.75 million in grants (from the Andrew W. Mellon Foundation, the Davis Educational Foundation, and the Arthur Vining Davis Foundation) and earned interest to support the launch of the FCLD. Of this, $250,000 was for significant renovations to the bunker, including upgrading the HVAC and fire protection systems. Over time, more than $1 million was invested in compact shelving; the balance was used to support the operating costs of the FCLD in the early years when the three-person staff included a professional librarian as director. The director planned the optimal shelving strategy.

The FCLD opened in November 2002 when the first shipment of materials was received. Capacity of the site is now estimated at 550,000 volumes, based on actual shelving space and compact storage strategies. Items are stored by volume size, not by call number. The FCLD now holds about 519,000 volumes with additional capacity for about 31,000 volumes. At the recent rate of shipments from the five campuses, the facility will be filled in one year or less. Facing the prospect of rapid filling of the remaining space, restrictions were recently placed by the Five College Librarians Council on the items that may be contributed to the FCLD collection.

The FCLD has very strong holdings of commonly held print journals, such as those digitized by JSTOR and others. In 2006 the Five College Librarians Council established an affiliate membership to the FCLD that allows academic libraries to pay a modest annual fee to have the right to request facsimile or print copies and propose additions to the collections that might complete or extend collections contributed by the Five Colleges Libraries. Currently there are about 180 FCLC affiliate members from six states.

Knowing that the FCLD is approaching capacity, FCLC has received and discussed various proposals to expand the facility. In spring 2011, a study authorized by the Five Colleges Board of Directors determined that it is not feasible to expand the FCLD at the bunker site. Alternatives are being explored. The ongoing need for storing little-used materials continues proportionately at all campuses, and all campuses continue to support the policy of placing such materials in the facility under the no-duplication, common use policies of the current depository. In November 2012, the Board of Directors endorsed continued exploration of expanding the facility.

Building on the FCLD affiliate member concept, FCLC has led discussions exploring the possibility of expanding the FCLD into a New England/North East Regional Depository (NERD). Discussion questions included:

- Are there other academic libraries willing to participate in a regional shared print collection, made up of monographs as well as journals, in which ownership rights are assigned to the shared collection?
- Is there a need for proprietary storage of institutionally owned, little-used materials?
- Is there a regional need for storage of other materials such as manuscripts, art, and other artifacts?

Before moving forward with a shared regional physical depository for monographs, several questions must be addressed:

- What is unique?
- Is this a dark archive, where items can't be accessed by users? If not, how can we guarantee a copy will always be available?
- How quickly can we provide access to an item for our faculty and student users?
- How does this fit into the national or international picture?
- How many copies do we need to keep?

The shared print collection of the Five College Libraries Depository is an extremely successful example of library cooperation and collaboration. The FCLD has preserved access to little-used print journals, and to a lesser extent, monographs, while eliminating unnecessary duplication among the Five Colleges Libraries and the affiliate members. Although there is definitely a need to expand the FCLD to include more print journal runs, the challenge will be to determine how well this model extends to collecting and preserving little-used monographs.

Notes

1. Willis E. Bridegam, "A Collaborative Approach to Collection Storage: The Five-College Library Depository," (Washington, D.C.: Council on Library and Information Resources, June 2001).
2. Neal Abraham, "Five College Library Depository: Background and Issues," Executive Director of Five Colleges Internal memorandum, November 26, 2012.

2CUL: A Case Study in Research Library Shared Staffing

Anne R. Kenney and James Neal

Need

- expand content coverage and provide deep subject expertise to support global collections in a joint capacity
- enhance access to research collections through shared delivery and borrowing privileges
- improve efficiencies from integration of technical services operation

Benefit

- build complementary global collections
- designate subject experts to acquire materials and provide in-depth research services for both institutions
- enhance access to the two collections through expedited delivery and on-site borrowing privileges
- securing faculty support and enthusiasm for these arrangements
- exercising collective bargaining in developing a Chinese

purchasing/shelf-ready plan in collaboration with Hong Kong
University and a Chinese vendor in Beijing

- analyzing digital preservation coverage for e-journal literature
and discovering that only 20 percent of our e-journal holdings
are in a trusted third-party archive
- investigate 2CUL e-book purchasing plans
- achieve flexibility in technical services by leveraging local
talent and skills, eliminating some workflow redundancies,
jointly purchasing some materials and services, and developing a web-based tool to automate much of the ordering
process
- conduct a project scoping analysis to determine the feasibility
and timing of a shared Library Management System (LMS)
- establish a 2CUL financial framework for tracking savings,
costs incurred, costs avoided, and reinvestments made on
both a recurring and one-time basis

Columbia University Libraries and Cornell University Library
entered into a bold partnership in 2009, dubbed 2CUL, a play on
their respective initials. 2CUL is a deep collaboration for providing
enhanced collections, resources, and services to faculty and students at
both institutions. The Andrew W. Mellon Foundation generously supported
the first phase of 2CUL (2009–2012).

Perhaps the most significant accomplishment of Phase 1 was building joint capacity to expand content coverage and provide deep subject
expertise to support global collections. By pooling resources and limiting
duplicative purchases, 2CUL has broadened the range of collecting in Asia,
Latin America, and Russia/Eastern Europe. Equally significant has been the
appointment of curators who serve both institutions in these areas. Two
curators are situated at Columbia, where we share a curator for Russia/East-
ern Europe and a curator for Latin America. The third curator, for Southeast
Asia, is at Cornell's distinguished Echols Collection on Southeast Asia.

In 2CUL Phase 1, our collective collection efforts took advantage of
the existing staffing situation. One institution's global resource area had
staff vacancies, and one had subject experts who were capable of managing

both collections and reference needs. We will consider three levels of deeper collection integration in Phase 2 (2013–2015). These efforts will be informed by our formal collection and usage analysis work, which will define the strengths of the respective 2CUL collections. On that basis we will set integration targets according to the following scale (with level 1 being the most integrated):

Integration Level 1: Integrated 2CUL Collection. One subject expert manages both CUL collections and the collection is integrated with minimal overlap for prospective acquisitions. In this case, one of the libraries may have a more extensive program than the other, and so one person will serve the particular subject needs (both collection development and in-depth reference) for both institutions. We are currently using this model for Slavic/ Eastern European studies and Latin American studies. For Southeast Asia, one institution does not have a significant program in that subject, so the other institution serves as a resource for in-depth reference or instructional needs that arise.

Integration Level 2: Coordinated 2CUL Collection. Subject experts at both schools consult closely to shape complementary collections. In this case, there are significant programs at both schools, and therefore subject experts are positioned in both libraries. The collections and in-depth reference services are managed jointly by the experts at each university in order to focus on localized needs and reduce unnecessary redundancy. This is currently in place for our Southeast Asian studies programs.

Integration Level 3: Separate Self-Standing Collections. In this case there are very strong, critical programs at each school, and while some collaboration will be considered, it will not be a prime focus. For instance, Cornell's agriculture collection is very strong, and Columbia will be able to rely on it to support its academic program focus on global sustainability.

Phase 2 collective collection actions will also focus on shared licensing, digital projects, shelf-ready cataloging, shared-buying trips, and a closer integration of collection analysis and use metrics to inform the collective collection.

Building joint collections and sharing subject specialists is becoming more commonplace, and one can point to the success of such coordination in the University of California system, the Committee on Institutional Cooperation (CIC), and the Triangle Research Libraries Consortium, among others. If this were all that Columbia and Cornell envisioned in terms of shared staff, there would be little to distinguish 2CUL as a distinctive new model.

The first phase of the 2CUL partnership sharpened our understanding of the critical importance of deep vertical integration. 2CUL involves a large number of staff as a means to achieve economies of scale, build capacity, and create the enabling infrastructure to advance the partnership broadly across the two library systems. An area that has proved particularly intractable to deep collaboration is technical services, a function that currently involves many staff engaged in high-volume, duplicative activities that are also characterized by institutional distinctiveness and local practices. At present, technical services operations represent a little over 20 percent of the respective staffs of both Cornell and Columbia libraries.

The second phase of 2CUL (2013–2015), again funded in part by The Andrew W. Mellon Foundation, is ambitious in scope and depth. Building an integrated technical services operation will be based on two key objectives:

1. Reconceiving operations at each library to achieve integration across both campuses by realigning staff responsibilities, workflow processes, and reporting lines to reflect an integrated operation

2. Ensuring that all technical services staff on both campuses understand and embrace 2CUL as an institutional goal and view inter-institutional collaboration as part of normal library operations

Three functions in particular are ripe for integration: ordering new library acquisitions; licensing and providing access to electronic resources; and automated import, export, and maintenance of catalog data. Integrating operations in these areas will yield an appreciable reduction in the staff resources required to handle current levels of this work and will permit us to reallocate needed resources to new and evolving areas of focus within technical services. Areas under consideration include nontraditional metadata support for faculty projects and research, research data curation, support for other digital library initiatives, and further innovations in processing

We also hope to bolster support for services in other divisions of the library, such as collection development and the enhancement and maintenance of library resource discovery systems. Further, the creation of a 2CUL cataloging department within a merged technical services operation will immediately increase the scope of staff language and subject expertise for both institutions—skills that are crucial to fruitful and effective bibliographic access to our collections—as well as increase opportunities to engage in cost-recovery processing for other institutions lacking in this expertise. Finally, the operational integration of these two large divisions of Columbia and Cornell libraries will influence and help to sustain the mainstreaming of 2CUL across both institutions.

Both institutions believe that building an integrated technical services operation is critical for consolidating the partnership, supporting deeper combined collections, and developing new capabilities for meeting new needs. It will require work on a number of fronts, including:

1. A thorough and systematic review of all existing technical services policies, practices, and workflows at each institution, with a view towards reconciling them as much as possible

2. Development of 2CUL best practices, guidelines, and policies to undergird the integrated operation

3. A redefinition of job responsibilities reflecting cross-institutional organizational structures through which unnecessary redundancy can be eliminated and workflows harmonized to serve Cornell and Columbia jointly

4. The reassignment/redeployment of staff at each institution to expand capacity in new areas

5. The identification of competencies needed for success in this new environment and the requisite training and development opportunities for staff at both institutions

6. The adoption of a new organizational/reporting structure and culture

7. The creation of a formal 2CUL framework through which we can exercise joint bargaining power when negotiating with vendors and other third parties for services and content

Many aspects of technical services integration can be planned and tested within the separate systems currently used by Cornell and Columbia. Work completed in Phase 1 provides some examples. To enable Cornell staff to catalog Korean books for Columbia, we first had to agree on common workflow, procedures, and standards, requiring some change and compromise from both institutions. We then implemented a virtual machine approach that allows the cataloger's workstation at Cornell to access Columbia's Voyager database. As a second example, the Pre-Order Online Form (POOF) created in Phase 1 allows a selector to use a single input to initiate orders in both Columbia's and Cornell's Voyager system.

As we work to integrate management of electronic resources, our common use of SerialsSolutions systems will allow staff to maintain data for both libraries in a combined operation. We intend to extend these strategies to incorporate broader and more flexible access to each other's Voyager environments, to further develop additional locally shared software, and to continue to search for vendor-supplied solutions to joint data maintenance problems as we begin to harmonize procedures and develop best practices for working together. These and new techniques that will emerge in the process can be employed more extensively as we begin to harmonize procedures.

The full benefits of technical services integration (TSI) will only be realized, however, when we are able to implement a common library management system that integrates data and workflows now occurring through separate software components. At this time, our explorations with various vendors and projects give us enough confidence to plan towards an implementation in 2015, but we will need to continue monitoring developments over the next two years and adjust plans accordingly. If new system readiness appears to be delayed, we will make more extensive use of the innovative techniques and workarounds noted above to realize benefits of staff and workflow integration within the next three years. On the other hand, if we see satisfactory progress towards new system implementation, we will do the necessary integration planning in advance but implement major changes only within the combined system.

We imagine a fully integrated technical services operation in which integration means that both campus units are part of a whole, specialization or particular functions are conducted at one campus on behalf of both libraries, and workflows are similar so as to support work sharing. For example, when one campus faces a backlog in technical processing, the other campus can pick up some of that work. We expect to realize efficiencies in selection and ordering of print and electronic resources, in data management for e-resources, in management of batch processing, in systems administration, and in more efficient use of specialized language and subject expertise.

Measurement of the collective full-time staff needed to perform specific functions before and after integration will provide concrete evidence of savings achieved and the ability to repurpose staff for emerging needs. This ambitious initiative will demand significant input from and discussion among current 2CUL staff under the direction of integration managers, who have been assigned at each institution.

The success of an integrated technical services operation will depend in large part on building a 2CUL culture that permeates the respective staffs at Columbia and Cornell. Phase 1 provided valuable lessons to guide this effort. The first lesson is: collaboration takes time. What may make sense conceptually does not translate easily into a shift in the way things are done. Change can be hard on staff, and they need to be supported in making the transitions and developing an understanding of the gains to be made. Second, cultural differences between Columbia and Cornell must be accommodated. Columbia Libraries has unionized staff; Cornell does not. Cornell faculty is more directly involved than Columbia faculty in changes affecting library operations. Third, for 2CUL to be fully integrated into the respective cultures of each institution, it has to be seen as providing more, not less, in terms of services, efficiencies, quality, responsiveness, and access to scholarship. Cost savings and economic challenges may have motivated the partnership, but they will not sustain it.

Mainstreaming 2CUL at the staff level in technical services will depend on integrating the 2CUL mission, vision, goals, and values into the staff's everyday thinking and action at all levels across the two libraries. It is important that all staff be fully aware of 2CUL's benefits and progress so that this shift in thinking and action can happen. Developing and implementing a staff engagement and communication plan to manage the transition to a different way of getting work done will be key to success. It will be critical to collect information about staff concerns/buy-in to the 2CUL model of collaboration and to engage staff at all levels and across the two libraries in the problem-solving process. This will tie their investment to the intended outcome of the collaboration. It also will be critical to secure the influence of the most effective opinion makers.

Another area in which we see great promise in terms of staffing is in technology innovation. In the second phase of 2CUL, Cornell and Columbia will explore a deeper level of technology innovation and collaboration across these three areas: major systems and services, platform and infrastructure, and pilot and "opportunistic" projects.

Major systems and services likely to require increased collaboration include integration and enhancement of a next-generation library system to support Technical Service Integration, innovation in search and discovery, and development and exploration of web archiving. Cornell and Columbia, along with several peer institutions, are developing technology infrastructure around systems including Fedora, Hydra, VIVO, and DPN. We expect to continue to share knowledge and increase our cooperation and collaboration related to digital preservation, repositories, data management, and forensics. Finally, technology teams from Cornell and Columbia will continue to seek out innovative projects that can leverage our respective expertise and enable new types of services, such as our recent collaboration on student newspapers, and potential projects related to research data and virtualization.

These objectives to integrate functions and share staff are necessary but insufficient to guarantee the long-term success of 2CUL. The collaboration must be understood and embraced beyond library walls. It will need to become an embedded partnership that is supported at the highest administrative levels of the two universities, within the campus communities, and throughout the library organizations. In sum, the major benefits of 2CUL will accrue once both institutions build and sustain a new and innovative research library future based on deep collaboration. The Technical Services integration and staff mainstreaming project will allow the two partners to engage all these issues in a significant division of library operations and will serve as a model for other institutions wishing to pursue similar partnerships.

Human Resources Management: Contractual Staffing at a Library Consortium

Lisa Priebe

Need

- a nongovernmental organization to accept payment for services so that funds are not absorbed back into the general state budget at the end of the year
- a fiscal agent to be the official employer of record for State Library staff
- a second contract to provide office space for contracted employees and space for associated computer servers with proper security and high-speed Internet access

Benefit

- strengthen ties with partner organizations
- collect administrative fees for fiscal management and human resources services
- comply with legal requirements for library services
- share cost of office space, equipment, Internet

As a nonprofit 501(c)(3), The Colorado Library Consortium (CLiC) has the ability to collect and manage funds for outside organizations. (See Case Study 16, Consortial Fiscal Sponsorship for more information.) In addition to providing fiscal management services, CLiC is in a position to provide human resources support for outside organizations. The Colorado State Library approached CLiC with such a request after another library consortium that was providing these services closed their doors. The State Library could not create new positions within the state government infrastructure, and it preferred that these employees report through a contractual relationship with an outside organization such as CLiC.

Several key statewide services would be impacted without such an arrangement. These included:

- Colorado Historic Newspaper Collection, a pre-1923 digitized collection of local newspapers
- AskColorado: a 24/7 virtual reference service staffed by after-hours employees
- SWIFT: a statewide ILL requesting and tracking system

These services are maintained on a group of servers owned by the State Library. Four employees either support the hardware infrastructure or the project's services, and the State Library needed to find an employer of record. In addition, the State Library was seeking a physical location to house the servers and the employee who maintains the equipment.

There were many human resources and business-related areas to consider before entering into such an arrangement. One major human resources management concern was how the benefit package compared to that of the previous consortium employer. After conducting a review and comparison, the benefits were found to be comparable. Another issue was hiring employees who would need part-time, temporary status. A large number of part-time employees are hired to work on an hourly basis to provide support for virtual reference through AskColorado. The State Library had internal reasons for not hiring employees with this status; however, as a nonprofit CLiC is able to hire using this employment status.

Under the agreement reached with the State Library, employees are managed by a State Library supervisor. Salary structure and pay increases are independent of those that other CLiC employees receive. Reviews and reprimands are handled using State Library processes and procedures.

Under this new contractual arrangement, CLiC grew from a staff of 9 to 35, which had a significant impact on human resources administration. A new payroll software system was adopted that streamlined payroll processing and allowed CLiC to take on the additional administrative work without needing to add support staff. CLiC standardized the orientation packet and sent information to new employees in advance. The employees who worked from home only needed to come to the CLiC office once to turn in the paperwork, review the employee handbook, and receive training on the payroll system. When an employee leaves, all termination tasks are completed by e-mail. All employee records are retained per state and federal laws.

One concern was that the addition of so many new employees would subject CLiC to additional employment laws for larger organizations. Research indicated that most federal and state employment laws become mandatory when an organization reaches 50 or more employees.

In addition to human resources, office space was also impacted by the decision to become a fiscal agent for the State Library. CLiC's office space was not large enough to accommodate the addition of a new employee and a server room. A benefit of sharing locations was that some office services costs could also be shared. CLiC negotiated for a larger office space that included the construction of a secure server room. All costs associated with the construction of the server room were borne by the State Library. All other construction expenses were paid for by CLiC.

Under the service agreement, the State Library pays a suite rental, which covers the cost of rent for an office and the server room, phones, and utilities. Since the State Library requires a more robust Internet connection, it also bears the cost for Internet service. The consortium is able to connect to the Internet for its own use. CLiC is able to house its own server in the secure room at no cost and may utilize the on-site expertise of the networking specialist.

CLiC also assists with contractual relationships. Any contract the State Library wishes to enter into to support the three services is negotiated by the State Library. CLiC reviews contracts and is the named party and signatory. The consortium maintains all paperwork associated with State Library contracts and makes sure all contractual obligations are met. It also creates and monitors invoices at the direction of the State Library. The State Library directs CLiC when bills should be paid. A State Library manager works closely with our office manager to maintain accurate and complete accounts. Reports are available upon request.

Each project is managed through a Memorandum of Understanding (MOU). An MOU outlines the responsibilities and timeframes for action of each organization for the areas mentioned in this case study. It outlines how changes to the agreement may be made, expiration or termination dates, confidentiality, and dispute resolution. An MOU is used in lieu of a formal contract as long as both parties agree that a less formal structure is in the best interest of both organizations. A sample of a memorandum of understanding can be found at www.nonprofitmaine.org/blob_view .asp?blob=28.

CLiC collects administration fees for each of the State Library MOUs. Because some MOUs require more work than others, a different fee structure is used for each MOU. In some cases it is a percentage of what we bill for payroll, benefits, and rental costs. In other cases it is based on an average number of invoices that CLiC will be requested to create and the number of bills to be paid.

The Human Resources Contractual Staffing arrangement has been in place since July 2010. There have been only minor adjustments to the agreements, and through cooperation and coordination, the relationship is working well for both parties.

BiblioTemps: A Temporary Employment Service for Libraries in Massachusetts

Kelly Jo Woodside

Need

- assistance with short-term staffing for member libraries
- opportunities for library workers to earn income, build experience, and stay connected to the profession during periods of unemployment or retirement
- alternative revenue streams for a library consortium

Benefits and Considerations

- helping members better serve their clientele
- addressing career development and library workforce needs
- strengthening ties to partner organizations
- developing a sustainable service model and infrastructure
- setting and meeting performance milestones

Staffing can be a significant challenge for library directors and boards. Vacations, medical leave, and unexpected vacancies frequently leave administrators scrambling to cover basic operations, while special projects may require investments of time or skills that existing staff cannot provide. At the same time, recruiting and screening candidates for temporary positions takes time away from other library functions, not to mention the logistical difficulty of processing a new hire in many organizations. Adding a direct hire in a municipality, for example, requires several layers of administrative approval—in some cases even a vote by town council. Barriers include complex recruiting guidelines and the need to include short-term direct-hire staff in employee fringe benefit plans. BiblioTemps clients, however, can bypass many of these requirements.

BiblioTemps® is a short-term staffing service for libraries that are members of the Massachusetts Library System (MLS).[1] Successfully operated by our predecessor organization from 2005 to 2009, the service was relaunched by MLS in May 2012 in response to member requests to help meet staffing needs. By the end of the first year, we had placed 46 Biblio-Temps in 28 libraries, filling 77 assignments ranging from single substitute circulation desk shifts to full-time multimonth interim director positions.

To participate, a member library first completes a client service agreement that outlines the terms of service, such as payment and invoicing, confidentiality, and liability. Then each time the library has an assignment, it simply submits a request-for-personnel form with the schedule, duties, pay rate, and other relevant details about the position. The BiblioTemps manager searches the staff database for candidates who match the client's needs, location, and schedule, and if necessary, recruits additional applicants. While we complete screening interviews and reference checks on all candidates, the client is invited to participate in the process by reviewing selected resumes as well as conducting on-site interviews with one to three final candidates. Thus the library is spared much time-consuming legwork but still gets to vet its temporary hire.

Some of our clients have even hired BiblioTemps employees permanently after successful short-term placements, thereby saving the time and expense of further recruiting. One way we differ from traditional temporary agencies is that we do not charge a conversion fee for permanent hires. Rather we view such hires as successful contributions to a healthy library workforce, thereby advancing the MLS mission to strengthen Massachusetts libraries.

Once placed, BiblioTemps are MLS employees; we process new hire paperwork, administer payroll, and invoice clients for the amount of the employee's wages plus a service fee. Employment laws and regulations are complex. We worked closely with MLS's business director and legal counsel to establish employment policies that, out of financial necessity, created a new class of temporary employee with a separate benefits package. Many clients find it easier to allocate budget funds for our services rather than to add a new hire directly, especially considering the daunting procedures required by some personnel departments. Short-term staffing solutions provided by BiblioTemps enable our members to better serve their patrons.

BiblioTemps is able to meet almost every client request because our service attracts a broad range of library workers. Those new to the profession face strong competition for entry-level jobs, so they are eager to build their library experience resume and networks through short-term assignments. In addition, many note a desire to use temporary work to explore the different work environments and roles available in our diverse profession. At the other end of the spectrum, we find recent retirees seeking opportunities to make use of their considerable experience and remain connected to the profession without the pressure or obligations of a permanent position. These retirees make excellent interim directors, which is one of our most common requests. In between are the library workers who have been displaced by budget cuts and downsizing, or who are seeking to supplement the part-time positions that are increasingly common at many libraries.

Working for BiblioTemps provides not only temporary income but also the opportunity to participate in MLS continuing education programs, which are normally offered only to staff in member libraries. In fact, we have added a series of career development webinars covering topics such as resumes, cover letters, and professional networking. By extending access to professional development opportunities for our staff, MLS is helping to ensure the strength of the library workforce in Massachusetts. In addition, we are able to identify potential issues to be addressed in future programs. For example, we've noted that some of the trustees we've worked with on interim director placements would benefit from more education about the recruiting and hiring process, so we are working to incorporate that into trustee orientation materials.

BiblioTemps has also helped fortify MLS's relationship with partner organizations. For example, we worked with the Simmons Graduate School of Library and Information Science to recruit new graduates for the service via campus career fairs and screening interviews. As a result, we've had opportunities to present in classes, meetings, and other events, where we can educate both students and faculty about not only BiblioTemps but the full range of MLS services. Early on, we found that library paraprofessionals was one of the harder communities to reach, so we also reached out to the Paralibrarian Section of the Massachusetts Library Association to help get the word out to their members about our employment opportunities.

Perhaps the most tangible benefit BiblioTemps provides MLS is the potential for a source of revenue. Although our service fees are considerably lower than those of for-profit temporary agencies, we hope that our service will help underpin the state-funded member services that MLS provides for free. Our goal was for BiblioTemps to become profitable within two years; however, it has been a challenge to determine profitability. Our revenue for the first year was triple what we had projected, and according to our original financial plan, we registered a positive net income. Nonetheless, during that year we realized that our plan had underestimated several key expenses, notably staffing time and payroll fees. An important goal in our second year has been to gather additional data to generate a more accurate financial analysis and to determine changes necessary to make Biblio-Temps a truly sustainable service.

Of course, the relaunch of BiblioTemps is the result of many months of planning and hard work, including:

- research and development of a business plan by MLS staff and board members
- recruiting and hiring a manager
- building an infrastructure including testing, selecting, and developing an automated applicant tracking system and online timesheet manager
- creating contracts, forms, and workflows for payroll and accounting
- designing a website and marketing materials

- doing outreach to library schools and organizations
- conducting hundreds of screening interviews to populate the initial candidate pool

Each of these processes involved a certain amount of trial and error, and most are continually being refined. For example, the current staffing plan includes a half-time manager as well as in-kind support from key MLS personnel in accounting, technology, and management. In reality, my time spent on BiblioTemps regularly exceeds the half-time allotment, and our in-kind support needs have evolved, so we are conducting a time audit to determine a more efficient model.

At the same time, we are planning further research to refine our performance assessment. In an MLS member satisfaction survey conducted during the first year of BiblioTemps, 89 percent of respondents rated the service four or five on a five-point scale of satisfaction. Although these numbers are promising, we would like to follow up with a more in-depth survey of our clients. Several additional milestones identified in the initial business plan, including target numbers for placements and revenue, were based in part on information from an earlier incarnation under our predecessor organization.

The library environment continues to evolve, so we need to account for changes as well as differing staffing models and resources. Ongoing research will ensure that we keep up with changes in the market. For example, we recently updated BiblioTemps pay rates so we can continue to attract competitive candidates, and we adjusted the service fee to more accurately reflect the resources required to operate the service. Next we hope to develop formulas to help us more accurately measure staff efforts on behalf of BiblioTemps, calculate projected revenue, and stay on target to build a sustainable service while maintaining a high level of member satisfaction.

Note

1. BiblioTemps® is a registered trademark of the Massachusetts Library System.

CASE STUDY 16

Consortial Fiscal Sponsorship

Valerie Horton

Need

- a grant requires fiscal agent with 501(c)(3) status
- an informal committee needs to pay an independent contractor
- a group of ILL librarians want to hold a conference and need to collect registration fees and pay for the event

Benefit

- cementing ties with partner library service organizations
- expanding capacity to serve consortium membership
- accessing website reservation systems and payment management systems
- providing fiduciary oversight
- collaborating to serve the mission and public relations goals of participating organizations

As a 501(c)(3) The Colorado Library Consortium (CLiC) can provide fiscal services to other groups under the Internal Revenue Service (IRS) rules for fiscal sponsors. Grantspace.org defines fiscal sponsorship as "a formal arrangement in which a 501(c)(3) public charity sponsors a project that may lack exempt status. This alternative to starting your own nonprofit allows you to seek grants and solicit tax-deductible donations under your sponsor's exempt status."

At this writing, CLiC handles the financial arrangements for over 20 groups, some informal and some more established. The consortium is seen as neutral territory where diverse groups can have access to administrative services at a minimal cost. If a group of libraries is planning an event, the consortium can provide a place where all participating libraries contribute as equal partners instead of having one library serve as the lead. To make use of this fiscal rule, the IRS requires that CLiC work closely with the group holding the event. Typically this means that one of the organization's regional consultants sit on the planning group and that there is a contractual relationship that spells out each party's role.

Why would an outside group wish to enter into a fiscal sponsorship with a 501(c)(3)? Some groups aren't sure they have the long-term viability to obtain and maintain their own 501(c)(3) status. Many informal groups find it easier to let an established consortium serve as the fiscal entity when they are planning a continuing education event. CLiC provides not only fiscal control but a registration system, contract negotiations and signing, conference planning assistance, and a website if needed. One example in Colorado is a group of librarians who have held over 30 interlibrary loan conferences. A long-standing group like this one may at some point wish to form their own 501(c)(3), but it may also wish to use CLiC's services to test the waters before deciding to go it alone. Other organizations that use CLiC's fiscal services include Colorado Libraries for Early Literacy, several regional conference groups, the special populations committee, and the State Library.

Another reason to seek 501(c)(3) fiscal sponsorships is to be able to submit a grant application. With grants, the consortium must be willing to be an active player in the entire grant process in order to meet the IRS fiscal sponsor rules. According to IRS rules, organizations that enter into a fiscal sponsorship relationship should be aware that the 501(c)(3) parent organization is legally responsible for all activities of the group. An example of a short-term grant project was a federal grant sought by a University of Colorado Libraries group that decided to digitize the Colorado Sanborn Fire Maps. The organization partnered with CLiC during the digitization, training, and website-establishment process. After all these tasks were completed, the group ceased to exist, and the University retained the digital project under its management.

Most organizations that allow fiscal sponsorships must have the arrangement approved by their governing board. When entering into a relationship, a memorandum of understanding can spell out what is required of each group and provide a clear distribution of assets if the partnership ends. The Colorado Resource Center has compiled a set of questions to consider before going into a fiscal sponsorship, which can be found at www.crcamerica.org/wp-content/uploads/2012/08/Fiscal-Sponsor.pdf.

There is some risk involved in a fiscal sponsorship arrangement. Legal responsibility for an event or project may fall on the fiscal sponsor, while full control may fall outside the consortium's control. Signatories to agreements on behalf of informal groups may be subject to personal liability risk due to lack of insurance and corporate standing. It is wise to verify insurance coverage under such arrangements. Financial responsibility may fall on the sponsor when a project ends up in the red.

Finally, what's in it for the consortium? If the missions of the group are similar to the consortium's interest, then both entities often can advance their goals more effectively by working together. For the consortium, the public relationship value of the partnership can be invaluable. For example, CLiC does not have the time or resources to provide extensive training in early childhood development, but by partnering with a group of experts in this area, they can make an important impact at minimal cost in resources. Finally, if every group of librarians in the state were to form nonprofit organizations, it could create serious confusion and perhaps, detrimental competition. Overall fiscal sponsorships have served the consortium well by helping to cement the consortium's reputation as a valuable contributor in many areas of librarianship in the state.

Conclusion

In this book we have attempted to capture the spectrum of services offered by library consortia in the current economic environment following the Great Recession. We were impressed during our research by the range of services offered by consortia today as well as the many innovative pilot projects underway. For example, the Massachusetts Library System is piloting three different e-book delivery systems to determine the best method of providing e-book access to member libraries. The SUNY libraries' e-textbook experiment is attempting to find a viable and sustainable path for libraries to provide a publishing function for their campuses. These are just two of many innovative initiatives taking place in library consortia.

Our goal was to capture the current reality of library consortia, both the bad (fiscal difficulties) and the good (innovation and a focus on crucial library needs). We wanted to conclude the book on a more personal note. We have more than 70 years of experience in libraries and 35 years working in five different consortia. In that time, we have learned a number of lessons that we wanted to share. We believe that our experiences will be especially valuable to new consortia directors, and they may also help experienced directors, as demonstrated by the lesson Greg learned on consolidating consortia. The next two sections are our personal statements about the field of consortia management.

Consortia Management as a Personal Journey

VALERIE HORTON

What does it take for a consortium to survive in turbulent periods? James Wiser in *Theological Librarianship* argues that there are three things: (1) a reliable source of funding, (2) a strong personality to lead the consortia, and (3) good timing.[1] Wiser has succinctly captured a complex topic. Evidence presented in this book clearly demonstrated that funding is the major issue impacting library consortia today. This is not a subject to take lightly considering the fact that over 65 consortia closed their doors in the last few years.

As I write this conclusion, I am starting my second year as director of Minitex, after working for eight years as director of the Colorado Library Consortium (CLiC). CLiC was created in 2004 after the first wave of regional system closures in the downturn following the bursting of the dot-com bubble and the September 11th attacks. Colorado lost seven regional systems in that economic crisis and had just enough state funding left to keep one system, CLiC, open to serve the entire state. This was not a small task given both the state's size and its more than 10,000 mountain passes.

Reliable Funding

In essence, CLiC was created out of a fiscal disaster, and that event impacted the organization through its formative years. In my first five years as director, I attended hundreds of meetings, and at every meeting library staff raised fears about the stability of CLiC's funding. It took years to settle the question in most people's minds, but in my eight years there it never did go away completely.

CLiC's funding changed over the years. Originally it was funded primarily by the state, but now only about one-third of the organization's revenue comes from state sources. The rest of the revenue comes from libraries choosing to support the organization's services such as the delivery system, an open-source integrated library system, continuing education events, and cooperative purchases including the statewide database package. Other revenue comes from a series of grants and from contracts with the Colorado State Library. Because CLiC is a 501(I)(3) corporation, we were also able to build a substantial reserve.

Each year, the CLiC Board and I updated our close-down plan. Fortunately, state funding remained stable and even increased during that time, so we never had to use that plan. The plan looked a lot like those undertaken by other consortia that have scaled back recently in that CliC would have cut any service that didn't make money. So consulting, continuing education, and a lot of marketing and advocacy work would have been lost, and it would have meant the loss of top-notch employees who had made CLiC a success.

I came to one very difficult realization during those years. Our state funding was not impacted by how well-managed CLiC was, or how great the staff was, or how valuable our services were to our member libraries. Our state funding was impacted more by national economic conditions and Colorado politics than it was by the quality of the organization's work. That knowledge still stings today. One takeaway from this realization is the need for a consortium to develop a means to generate support when legislative advocacy for funding support is required. CLiC is now under a new director and is doing great, with state funding remaining solid.

In 2012, when I went through the hiring process at Minitex, one of the questions I frequently was asked was how I would ensure the sustainability of Minitex funding. This question was not a surprising in light of nationwide consortia closings, but it was somewhat unexpected given that Minitex has one of the most stable financial structures of any consortium operating in the United States today. I fear that it will take decades of funding stability before library staff can again trust in the future of their consortia. I find this concept dangerous, because the very fear of losing funding could cause libraries to choose not to participate in the organization's service, thereby creating a self-fulfilling prophecy.

Another realization I came to over time was the need to remain positive when members dropped one of our services. If you look at the history of library consortia, member libraries have joined and dropped out, and then rejoined a few years later. Given the fear operating in our profession these days, many managers are becoming too stringent in their response to the very normal occurrence of a library threatening to leave a cooperative. In the end we need to remember that our service participation and memberships will always be fluid. We must build our systems to entice people to join or rejoin, and not give in to the short-term thinking that argues that if we can punish those who leave, they'll stay with us. I have learned to trust the truism that carrots always work better than sticks in the long run.

Leadership

Which brings me to Wiser's second point: consortium leadership. Leadership is difficult to write about; sometimes I think it is like great art and you know it when you see it. I have seen great consortia leaders in my time. Bill DeJohn, the former director of Minitex, surely qualifies as does John Helmer at OrbisCascade, Randy Dykhuis at the Midwest Collaborative for Library Services, Ann Okerson at the Center for Research Libraries, and too many others to name here. But what makes these people great leaders?

I once asked a retired Colorado regional system director, Lorena Mitchell, why she was so well-regarded in the library community. Her answer, "I always showed up." It's as simple as that! A good consortia director shows up at lots of events, such as a library opening, training events, and conferences. This list includes events not sponsored by the consortium. A good consortium manager has a lot of miles on his or her car.

I don't think Lorena only meant physically showing up, however. I think she also meant that a good leader is out in the field to listen and learn from the consortium's stakeholders. I believe that the most important thing in library work is our relationships with each other. Relationships are built upon understanding, listening, open discussion, and active engagement with our colleagues.

A good leader must have all the standard management skills, such as good personal skills, a willingness to be tough and make unpopular decisions when necessary, and a solid knowledge of the fundamentals of the library profession. But a leader is more than a good manager. I think a leader must be a risk taker. Sometimes that means taking on more work than the organization can handle, knowing, or perhaps more accurately taking a reasoned chance, that the resources will be found to make the new services or projects work. Sometimes that plan doesn't work; Randy Dykhuis's case study illustrates such a circumstance.

Sometimes leadership is getting out there on a limb and seeing a whole new vision of how the profession can function. John Helmer's work at Orbis Cascade Alliance, combining the e-book collections of 37 independent academic libraries in the Pacific Northwest into one integrated collection, is an example of risk-taking that qualifies as transformational. Also consider the vision of a leaders like Dan Cohen from the Digital Public Library of America (DPLA). Cohen's belief in the power of the collaborative and in open access is so strong that his organization has prompted many existing digital libraries to rethink basic operating assumptions. Many digital libraries are moving from tightly managed collections to risk-taking, open ventures that are inviting our communities to be a part of the process, not just the recipient of the static information.

I can see that what I just wrote may appear paradoxical. How do you both listen and understand member needs and have the ability to see a whole new vision of the future of libraries that leads stakeholders to change? I believe the answer is that one informs the other. A consortium leader has to truly understand where libraries are today before a transformational new service can be cooperatively created.

There are many deep collaborative projects developing across the library community. These projects are examples of how listening and leadership have been merged by many in our profession, and they may be the most amazing thing I have witnessed in my 35-year career. Projects like DPLA, HathiTrust, or Kauli Ole prove the power of this concept. Libraries can no longer be islands. We have a newfound belief that we can build something new and better by gathering resources of money, materials, and talented people. Kudos to our profession!

Good Timing and Luck

Earlier I mentioned my distress that so much of consortial funding is based on national economics and state politics, which are largely out of the control of a consortium's leader. I did not mean to imply that any consortium would survive without being well run and providing value for member libraries. Clearly, without the widespread support and participation from the library community, no consortium would retain membership or funding. That means the consortium director must run a great organization, thereby generating advocates for funding. But we must also be lucky. So back to Wiser's third point, that library consortia need good timing as well as a working economic system to thrive.

Good timing is related to the nation's economics and to library trends, but it also has another component—the crucial ability of a leader to know when to jump on a new service bandwagon. When CLiC was first formed it had four services: delivery, continuing education, consulting, and cooperative purchases. Over eight years, as opportunities came up, we added an open-source online catalog system and two public library e-book collections, took on a human resource management function, become a fiscal entity for other organizations, and added management of Colorado's major database package.

Each of those projects had a critical timing component as part of the decision. Is this the right time to add a new service? Is the service important enough to members that they will contribute to its financial sustainability over the long term? In reality, it is rare that circumstances will tell a manager that now is the time to expand. We always have overworked staff, too little money, and inadequate resources to launch new services. Many times to grow there is no choice but to jump and then fix the system so that the new project can be integrated into existing operations after the fact. Juggling like this is not easy, but it is necessary.

Right now, in my opinion, the library as publisher is a crucial evolution for libraries and supporting consortia. Statewide database and e-book packages have created huge, homogenized collections that make every library look just like every other library. Homogenized collections are great in terms of equalizing access but bad in terms of showing the reason why any given library exists. Further, traditional book circulation is dropping across all types of library users, and some library thinkers argue that books have become so cheap and easy to find that they are now commodities. Commoditization is never a good thing, and like homogenized collection, this trend raises the question of the overall value of a library to its funders.[2]

I foresee Minitex taking a role in supporting libraries as they serve patrons by capturing unique, local, and primary source materials. The key value there is local, and it doesn't matter whether the materials are county government publications, photography collections, personal narratives or poems, genealogies, or local history materials. Libraries have a role in the crucible of creation, and this new service will be messy and confusing for some time as we explore this next great library mission. Is this the right role for Minitex? I hope so, but I am not clairvoyant, so watching for other key issues will remain a critical part of my work.

In conclusion, I believe Wiser is correct. We must diversify our funding streams and work to convince our library stakeholders that our financial future is on firm ground. We must not just nurture strong leaders, we must also develop strong consortium employees at every level. Finally, we must be lucky. To quote a line from the musical *Pippin*, "It's smarter to be lucky, than it's lucky to be smart!"

Lessons Learned from Consolidation
Greg Pronevitz

This book arose out of our interest in learning how library consortia weathered the storm of the 2008–2009 world economic crisis. I experienced an earlier smaller storm in 2004 when Massachusetts regional library systems sustained an 18 percent budget cut following the recession of the early 2000s. It resulted in a small number of reductions in force and some service reductions across the six systems. The 2010 budget cuts exceeded 30 percent and resulted in a major consolidation and numerous layoffs. Some services were curtailed and others eliminated.

More Mergers are Possible

Consortia in eight states have experienced two major rounds of consolidation in the past decade. The five Massachusetts consortia comprised six percent of the 79 consortia that closed their doors between 2003 and 2013 following these recessions. While the experience was a serious challenge to participants and libraries, the results include some benefits. It is possible that more states will go through this reduction in library services. I'd like to note some considerations for others who may need to go through this process.

The 2008–2009 economic crisis became personal to me when the magnitude of the cuts in Massachusetts became clear and we had to face the fact that we would shrink from six independent regional library systems to one or two systems. Planning began with discussions between our state library agency and library leaders throughout the state. Emotions among regional library system staff ran high with the realization that many positions would need to be eliminated. Some member library staff members with strong loyalties to their local regional library systems also responded emotionally.

The Massachusetts consolidation was guided by a transition committee comprised of board members from each of the six regions, the six regional administrators, and the director of the state library agency. A decision was reached to consolidate the six systems into a single system at a statewide meeting of all board members of all systems. The decision was not unanimous; a majority of voters prevailed. The committee met regularly for several months. The group drafted a budget and plan of service for the new statewide system. Again, the decisions were not by consensus and some decisions were not unanimous.

The transition committee created a hiring group to build the staff roster for opening day. Preference was given to existing staff. Applications were accepted only from current employees of the existing systems. Positions were offered to a number of regional library system employees to create an opening day staff to fulfill the plan of service within budget. The executive director's position was handled separately by the newly appointed board of directors and included a national search.

Simultaneously with system planning, each system was winding down operations in consultation with an attorney. The winding-down process included disposal of assets that would not be needed by the new system, planning for severance, canceling contracts and leases, gathering corporate records, and shipping records. Assets and corporate records were transferred to the two offices of the new system that would remain open, and there was a gap in communications with members until decisions could be made public.

I was hired as executive director 26 days prior to the launch of the new system. It was a busy month! Two key positions were vacant on opening day. Deferring to the executive director, the board had decided not to hire an assistant director. And because none of the former business managers or bookkeepers applied for a position with the successor organization, no bookkeeper was on staff. Now three-plus years after the transition, we are in very good shape. I do have some recommendations for anyone contemplating a consortial merger:

- Hire a facilitator to work through the not-for-profit merger planning process. Mergers can be fraught with conflict, emotion, and complex decisions. Ask your planning group to come to consensus on the process, if possible.

- Appoint or hire a caretaker director to oversee the transition operations as a watchdog for the new organization. Our winding-down process was rushed at times and decisions about what to retain and how to treat some assets and corporate records were disorganized without a dedicated decision maker.

- Hire an attorney who is experienced with mergers. Seek advice to minimize future legal obligations. A merger of corporations makes the successor corporation responsible for the actions of the predecessor organizations. It may be possible to simply close down corporations that are no longer needed. One challenge we faced immediately after our merger was an Internal Revenue Service partial audit of one predecessor organization. We were unable to locate a key document. The legal expenses and level of internal effort to get through the audit were high. Such distractions are not conducive to organizational development.

The pros and cons of owning real estate was another lesson learned. In my career at library consortia, I've worked in six different offices. Most of them were leased space in an office building. However, I have also worked in two buildings that were owned by a consortium. There are pros and cons to owning real estate, or should I say, co-owning real estate with your mortgage lender. After these experiences my personal preference is to avoid the long-term commitment and associated risks and responsibilities. I prefer to accept the alternative risks and benefits that come with the shorter-term commitment of leasing space.

The benefits of being an owner become most apparent when the mortgage is paid off. The bill just disappears. The need to renegotiate your lease with your landlord disappears. The facility can be modified to match your specifications. Member library staff and your own employees become familiar with and attached to the place. It can help build a sense of community. If you have surplus space, your consortium can lease it and derive some income. You become less susceptible to upward price swings in the commercial real estate market. Another reason to own is when acceptable rental space is not available.

In light of these advantages, why would I prefer to be a tenant? First, as we have learned, the chief determinant of a consortium's financial future is the overall economy, not the efficiency of the organization. When the overall economy goes sour, the real estate market is likely to go with it. If you need to sell the building or find tenants to cover your costs, that need is most likely to arise when it is most difficult to execute. The second reason to rent is that it allows a consortium to focus on providing services to libraries. Facilities management, renovations, and other obligations related to being a landlord are an ongoing distraction. Renewing a lease and negotiating improvements once every three to five years seems preferable to me.

Difficulty in predicting the future is reason number three. Owning real estate is a long-term responsibility. When you buy or build for your anticipated long-term needs, are you certain that in 15–20 years that your forecast will have been correct? As libraries shift from owning and lending traditional books and media to focusing more on electronic resources and becoming a community space, will consortial spaces shift too? Staff are telecommuting more and spending less time in the office. How many consortial managers of now defunct organizations predicted mergers and/ or a shut down? Owned space is finite. It is likely to become too large or too small in the future.

The Silver Lining

The merger achieved measurable efficiencies in Massachusetts. The cost avoidance for member libraries increased by over 40 percent, with a return of about $15 in services for each dollar invested. We invested more in statewide online content, and that spending increased by 46 percent to expand access to these resources for all residents. I believe we are better positioned to empower libraries with their own transition from traditional content to e-content.

Statewide decision-making was simplified. This was exemplified by a quick reaction to members' call to action for a statewide e-book platform (see Case Study 3, Statewide E-book Project for Multitype Libraries in Massachusetts). As I noted in chapter 2, a major challenge to consortia is the ability to support large-scale resource sharing as e-content becomes a more important component of library collections. From my new statewide perspective I became acutely aware of the trend to provide e-content from silos that served only parts of the state. The volume of interlibrary loan and circulation of traditional library materials was stabilizing. I saw a risk to statewide resource sharing as the most significant challenge for Massachusetts libraries. I believe that decisive action on this scale would have been unlikely under the former structure.

A second example of statewide decision-making to benefit libraries was the consolidation of physical delivery. This step resulted in a contract with a single vendor and a leap forward in labor-saving technology, simplifying management at our consortium and processing in libraries as well as controlling costs. Strong buy-in to the old status quo and resistance to change among librarians may have prevented a statewide approach if the six consortia had not merged.

Working Together

I have seen benefits to increasing the scale of projects in Massachusetts. I feel it is my role to continue to identify potential efficiencies for libraries by working together. I also know our limitations, and I see areas where the scale of collaboration and development should be beyond a single state. There are important areas where joint efforts are justified.

The megaconsortia mentioned in chapter 2 have accomplished a great deal to help consortia and libraries operate effectively, collaborate, and move forward with technology.

As resource sharing and general circulation become more and more electronic, I hope that shared or centralized development of user-friendly technology and systems can help libraries meet their goals and some of the major challenges outlined in chapter 2, such as licensing and providing popular e-books to patrons, sharing physical and digital repositories, and employing interstate physical delivery.

Conclusion

The two narratives included in this chapter illustrate the complexity of library consortia management. Consortia are impacted by the national economic situation and have little direct influence over funding loss from governmental sources. However, it is clear that running streamlined, customer-focused organizations is within the manager's control and is crucial to consortial survival. This book attempts to provide guidance in the best practices for managing core consortia services and examples of innovations that may become part of our future.

It is also clear that this is a time of innovation and experimentation with deep collaborative projects for the library profession. Consortia managers are required to take risks with new projects and new ways of doing their work that are transforming the profession. Not only does a consortia director have to be a good manager, but he or she also needs to be a leader who shows member organizations the value of using collaboration to achieve better outcomes for library users.

We believe this was a critical time for writing a book on consortia management. Library consortia have come through a difficult time of closures, mergers, and retrenchment. We are now in a time of innovation and experimentation with new ways of doing our work. We hope this book helps guide those who work in consortia as well as those who are members of consortial organizations in navigating a new, fascinating era in library consortial change.

Notes

1. James Wiser, "Playing Well with Others: New Opportunities for Library Consortia," *Theological Librarianship* 4, no. 1 (2011).
2. Rick Anderson, "Can't Buy Us Love: The Declining Importance of Library Books and the Rising Importance of Special Collections," *Issue Brief*, www.sr.ithaka.org/blog-individual/cant-buy-us-love-rick-anderson-kicks-new-ithaka-sr-issue-briefs-series.

About the Authors and Contributors

Valerie Horton has been director of Minitex since December 2012. Minitex serves Minnesota, North Dakota, and South Dakota libraries with a large resource-sharing network, databases, continuing education, remote storage, and many other services. Horton is also the co–general editor for *Collaborative Librarianship*, and wrote *Moving Materials: Physical Delivery in Libraries* for ALA Publications. Prior to working at Minitex, she was the first director of the Colorado Library Consortium (CLiC), a statewide library service organization. Before CLiC, Valerie was Director of the Library at Mesa State College in Grand Junction for seven years. She came to Mesa State after ten years at New Mexico State University, where she was Head of Systems, and for a time, library budget director/associate director. During her tenure in New Mexico, Valerie received an ALA International Fellowship and spent a year in the Republic of Trinidad and Tobago, where she consulted on how to automate the country's public, school, and government libraries. She started her professional career as a systems librarian at Brown University in Providence, Rhode Island, after graduating from and working in Systems at the University of Hawaii.

Greg Pronevitz was appointed founding executive director of the Massachusetts Library System (MLS) in 2010 after budgetary pressures compelled the consolidation of six regional library systems. MLS serves more than 1,500 multitype members with physical delivery, shared e-content, training and professional development, consulting, mediated interlibrary loan and document delivery services. He speaks and writes in the areas of physical delivery service, shared online content, and digital libraries. Prior to the formation of MLS, Pronevitz had extensive experience as founding director, managing the provision of services to libraries in a consortial environment at the Northeast Massachusetts Regional Library System and as assistant director at OHIONET. His professional library experience includes positions in technical services at Ohio State University, Chemical Abstracts Service, and the Center for Research Libraries, where he began his career as a cataloger for Slavic materials. He received an MLS (including two semesters of study on a graduate student exchange with Moscow State University in the former Soviet Union) and a BA in Russian language and literature from the State University of New York at Albany.

Lori Bowen Ayre is a library consultant specializing in library delivery systems, materials handling, and all the technology and equipment that comes into play in optimizing these systems. She has written extensively about the use of RFID and is a frequent presenter on RFID as well as automated materials handling, interlibrary delivery, resource sharing, and open-source software. Ayre writes the Technology Matters column in *Collaborative Librarianship* and has contributed chapters to *Moving Mountains: Physical Delivery in Libraries* and *RFID-Applications, Security and Privacy*. She has also written two issues of *Library Technology Reports*. She received her master's degree in library and information science from San Jose State University in 2006.

Liz Bishoff is currently the owner and principal consultant for The Bishoff Group, a library and cultural heritage consulting services organization. Previously Bishoff was the director of Digital and Preservation Services at the Bibliographic Center for Research, where she worked closely with organizations as they developed and managed their digital program. Bishoff was also vice president for Digital Collection Services at OCLC and founding executive director of the Colorado Digitization Program. Under several IMLS National Leadership Grants, Bishoff led the development of collaborative best practices in metadata and digital imaging, resulting in the widely adopted CDP Metadata Dublin Core Best Practices and the Digital Imaging Best Practices.

Linda Crowe is the executive director of Califa Group, a statewide California library consortium. Califa is responsible for purchasing electronic resources, hardware, and software, and administrating the program for its 220 member libraries. She is also chief executive officer of the Pacific Partnership, a consortium covering eight California counties. The Pacific Partnership prepares and monitors the budget, organizes programs, and develops grant proposals. Crowe has been a member of the California Library Association since 1984 and has served as president. She earned her master's degree in library science at Case Western University.

Kathleen Drozd is assistant director of Minitex, which is located at the University of Minnesota, Twin Cities. Minitex is an information and resource-sharing program of the Minnesota Office of Higher Education and the University of Minnesota Libraries. Her responsibilities have included direction of the Minitex Delivery System, which serves Minnesota and the Dakotas. She also directs the Minnesota Library Access Center, a remote storage facility for 21 libraries. Drozd has served on the NISO Physical Delivery of Library Resources Working Group, which authored a best practices document published in January 2012.

Randy Dykhuis is executive director of the Midwest Collaborative for Library Services, a nonprofit membership organization that provides libraries in Michigan and Indiana with a convenient single point of contact for training, group purchasing, and technical support for electronic resources. He is the author of the 2009 article, "Michigan Evergreen: Implementing a Shared Open-source Integrated Library System," which was published in *Collaborative Librarianship*. In 2003, Dykhuis won Wayne State University's Distinguished Alumus award. He received his Master's in Library Science from Wayne State University, Detroit.

Jeanine F. Gatzke is a technical services librarian and associate systems administrator at Concordia University's St. Paul Library. She received her master's degree in library and information science in 2002 from Dominican University, River Forest, Illinois, in the joint program with the College of St. Catherine in St. Paul. She has served on a number of operational committees and communities of interest in all areas of technical services throughout her 18-year history with Cooperating Libraries in Consortium (CLIC).

Deborah Hoadley is advisor and team leader for the MLS Statewide eBook Pilot Project at the Massachusetts Library System in Marlborough. Her primary focus is strategic planning, leadership, collaborations/partnerships, and more recently, resource sharing. She is the president of the New England Library Association, where she is working to bring the six New

England states together to work cooperatively on resource-sharing projects. Hoadley has presented at local, state, and regional conferences on the areas of advocacy, planning, leadership, and consortial e-books. In 2011, she received the YWCA Tribute to Women Award for building strong connections between the public library, the town, and the community

Jennifer Hootman is coordinator of Reference Outreach & Instruction at Minitex. She works with library staff, educators, and students to provide instruction and support for the statewide e-resources. Her areas of interest and experience include the design and development of instructional materials and online tutorials, e-learning/teaching, instruction of first-year university students and students in grades 6–12, curriculum development, and professional development for library staff and educators. Hootman earned an MA in history at Illinois State University and an MLIS from the University of Illinois at Urbana-Champaign.

Anne R. Kenney is the Carl A. Kroch University Librarian at Cornell University in Ithaca, New York. Her research has focused on digital imaging, digital preservation, and more recently, collaborative organizational responses to 21st-century challenges. She is the coauthor of three award-winning monographs and over 50 scholarly articles and reports. Kenney is a fellow and past president of the Society of American Archivists and serves on the board of the Association of Research Libraries. She has received numerous awards for her research, teaching, and service to the profession. Kenney earned her master's degrees in history and library science at the University of Missouri.

Belinda E. Lawrence is the public access librarian at the St. Catherine University library. She received her master's degree in library science in 2002 from Dominican University, River Forest, Illinois. She has served on several committees in CLIC over the past 15 years and also participated in the migration and implementation of CLIC's shared ILS. Lawrence's research is concentrated on student employees and their role in libraries. She coauthored with Kate Burke the article "Accidental Mentorship: Library Managers' Roles in Student Employees' Academic Professional Lives," *College & Research Library News* 72 (February 2011): 99–103.

Matt Lee is a librarian at Minitex, where he provides online and in-person instruction on library databases and reference strategies. He works with library staff, educators, and students to build capacity in online research skills. Lee earned an MLIS degree from Dominican University/St. Catherine's University.

Tracey Leger-Hornby provides management consulting services with an emphasis on academic libraries and information technology systems. Prior to starting her consulting practice, Leger-Hornby served as dean of Library Services at Worcester Polytechnic Institute, associate CIO at Brandeis University, director of the Regina Library at Rivier College in Nashua, New Hampshire, and in various roles at the Simmons College Libraries. Leger-Hornby served on the board of trustees of the Northeast Regional Computing Program (NERCOMP) and held the offices of chair, treasurer, and secretary. She is co-chair of the ACRL New England Chapter Leadership Development Committee and was co-leader of the EDUCAUSE Professional Development Constituency Group, served on the EDUCAUSE Quarterly Editorial Board, and was a member of the FRYE Institute Class of 2003. Her doctoral research focused on women's attitudes toward computers and the implementation of technology in higher education.

Victoria Teal Lovely is the director of technology services at the South Central Library System in Madison, Wisconsin, where she manages the Koha ILS for 42 public libraries. Lovely served as the president of the Customers of Dynix, Inc., user group (CODI) and as secretary of the Koha Users and Developers of Open-Source (KUDOS). She has been a frequent presenter at the CODI conference, the Wisconsin Library Association Conference, WiLSWorld, and at ALA as a panel presenter on managing an open-source ILS in a consortium. Lovely earned her master's in library science at the University of Wisconsin, Madison.

James Neal is the vice president for Information Services and university librarian at Columbia University. He provides leadership for university academic computing and for a system of 22 libraries. His responsibilities include the Columbia Center for New Media and Learning, the Center for Digital Research and Scholarship, the Copyright Advisory Office, and the

Center for Human Rights Documentation and Research. Previously Neal served as dean of University Libraries at Indiana University and John Hopkins University, and he held administrative positions in the libraries at Penn State, Notre Dame, and the City Universities of New York.

Cyril Oberlander took the position as dean of the library at Humboldt State University in California in July 2014. Previously he served as director of Milne Library at the State University of New York at Geneseo. He was the principal investigator for the Open SUNY Textbook Project. Oberlander previously held positions as associate director of Milne Library and director of Interlibrary Services at the University of Virginia Library; Head of Interlibrary Loan at Portland State University, and in various roles in Access Services. Cyril's consultation experience includes independent consulting services and workflow design with various vendors and libraries. Research interests include organizational development, workflow design, publishing, information visualization, and knowledge systems.

Ann Okerson joined the Center for Research Libraries as senior advisor on electronic strategies in 2011, working with that organization to reconfigure and redirect various existing programs into digital mode. Her previous experience includes 15 years as associate university librarian for Collections & International Programs at Yale University, work in the commercial sector, and 5 years as senior program officer for scholarly communications at the Association of Research Libraries. Upon joining Yale, Okerson organized the Northeast Research Libraries Consortium (NERL), a group of 28 large and more than 80 smaller libraries negotiating for electronic information. She is one of the active, founding spirits of the International Coalition of Library Consortia (ICOLC).

Mary Parker is an associate director at Minitex. She manages the Electronic Library for Minnesota (ELM) and the Reference Outreach and Instruction programs along with other programs. Her professional interests involve continuing education and outreach, communication, and marketing of statewide services to audiences ranging from library staff, faculty and educators, students of all ages, and the public. Parker earned an MA in library science from University of Minnesota–Twin Cities.

Lisa Priebe is a project manager at the Colorado Library Consortium in Centennial, Colorado. Her experience has focused on improvements to resource sharing and customized software systems that streamline consortium operations. She has written articles for *Collaborative Librarianship* and was a contributor to *Moving Materials: Physical Delivery in Libraries*. In 2007 she received the Colorado Association of Libraries Technology Project award for the development of LEO: the Library Education Opportunity calendar. Priebe received her master's degree in library and information science from the University of Denver.

Jay Schafer has been director of libraries at the University of Massachusetts-Amherst since 2004. He combines his expertise in library collection building, resource sharing, and facilities space planning with a deep dedication to providing innovative, high-quality service to library users. The Learning Commons in the W.E.B. Du Bois Library is one successful example of his belief that libraries must evolve to meet the needs of today's students while maintaining the high standards expected of a nationally ranked research library. Schafer is currently a member of the executive board of the Association of Research Libraries and member of the board of trustees and treasurer of LYRASIS. He is past chair of the Five Colleges Librarians Council and past president of the Boston Library Consortium.

Mark Sullivan is the executive director of the IDS Project and helped to create the IDS Project in 2004 with Ed Rivenburgh as they travelled throughout New York State sharing the benefits of cooperative optimization, innovation, and mentoring libraries. Sullivan has also developed many tools used by IDS Project libraries and other libraries across the country. Some of his work includes: ALIAS, a highly effective article request system for IDS Project libraries that offers all libraries cooperative licensing data instrumental in making resources available; 18 ILLiad Addons; the Getting It System Toolkit; and other technologies that are widely used across 1,200 ILLiad libraries. Sullivan earned a BS in biology from Cornell University, a Juris Doctor from Vermont Law School, and an MLS from the University at Buffalo.

Heather Teysko is the assistant director of Innovation and Development at the Califa Library Group. She has been with Califa since 2005, helping member libraries save over $4 million each year in group purchases and spearheading new initiatives such as the annual The Edgy Librarian web conference. Teysko has a history of working with digital rights and licensing issues. Before joining Califa, she was the head of the Naxos Music Library for the Naxos record label (the world's largest classical label) and the first US staff member of Classical.com, now owned by Alexander Street Press, the world's first online streaming classical music database for libraries.

Kelly Jo Woodside is the manager of BiblioTemps® and an advisor for the Massachusetts Library System in Marlborough, Massachusetts. She recruits and places short-term library staff at all levels in multitype libraries throughout the state and provides consultation and continuing education on a range of library issues. Woodside earned her master's degree in library and information science from Simmons College in Boston, where she later worked as career resource librarian and taught the continuing education course "Revitalize Your LIS Career." In 2007 she helped found the Conference Career Center for the Massachusetts Library Association and coordinated it for several years. She has also served as information literacy librarian at Simmons and head of Reference and Information Literacy Services at Assumption College in Worcester, Massachusetts.

Index